THE WEST AUSTRALIAN MONDAY NOVEMBER 13 1989

22 THE WEST AUSTRALIAN MONDAY MAY 15 1989

Child migrants

By JENNY BERICH

MOST Australians aren't aware of it, but there are more than 50,000 people living here who were "forced emigrants".

They were Britain's child migrants. Now they are middle-aged Australians searching for an identity. In WA there are more than 10,000 of them.

From 1913 to 1983 the British Government took more than 250,000 children aged from three to 14 from England, Northern Ireland, Scotland, Wales and Malta and moved them to Canada, South Africa and Australia. The peak migration period was 1938 to 1957.

Lionel "Geordi" Welsh, of Carlisle, was 11 when he made the six-week boat trip from England to Australia in 1947.

He believed he was going to a land of milk and honey where children rode horses to school.

But a rude shock awaited when he was taken by bus to a place he described as "desolate": Boys' Town at Bindoon.

"It was snowing when we left England and it was more than 100 degrees when we arrived," he said.

"They stripped us of our clothes and issued us with khaki shirts and pants.

"I felt I had been conned."

After four years at Boys' Town Mr Welsh ran away, worked round Australia and eventually became a builder.

Although happy with his life, Mr Welsh always wanted to find his true identity. He wanted to know ...

Broth...

By MARA PRITCHA...

THREE brothers torn ... under the British-Aust... child migrant scheme 42 ... ago were reunited at the end.

The last time Maurice ... man, 50, and his b... Alan, 51, and Joe 53, ... gether was when Maur... Joe were boarding a ... take them to a ship be... Fremantle.

The three brothe... meant to come to Aus... gether but Alan failed ... ical test and was left b...

"I remember Alan trying to get on to the bus because he wanted to come with us but the nuns from the convent we were at pulled him away by his shirt collar and dragged him back inside," Joe said yesterday.

"They locked him inside a room and told him to start writing letters to his brothers in Australia."

Alan and his family flew into Perth on Saturday night and for the first time in 42 years the three brothers were together.

But the story of a family torn ... begin or end ...

...aurice Norman

...brothers are bitter about the child migrant scheme.

Alan is particularly bitter about being left behind.

"It is great to come to Perth and see my brothers but I feel though I am making a trip I ... made 42 years ...

"Both the British a... tralian governments hav... to answer for.

"They have the bloody cheek to lecture other countries about human rights when they put so many families like ours through the living hell that was the child migrant scheme.

"They lived a lie then and they are living it now because they don't want to know what ...ned to the thousands of ... lost."

...Advertiser, Friday, August 28, 1987 — 15

Transported ... for the crime of lacking a family

Thousands of orphaned and abandoned British children were sent to Australia, Canada and South Africa after World War II because they had no families to raise them. A trust has been set up to help the children — now grown into adults — to trace their backgrounds. Jill Rowbotham reports from London.

THE heirs to the social welfare policy which allowed children institutionalised because they had no family to raise them to be sent to Australia, Canada and South Africa are pained by it and defensive about it.

Last month the *London Observer* newspaper published the stories of adults who had been shipped to places all over Australia as children and who had been unhappy there.

That such a policy for placing children — in some cases splitting them from brothers and sisters — ever flourished seems incredible in today's climate which strongly emphasises fostering and adoption.

Three of the agencies involved were Dr Barnardo's, the Catholic Children's Society and the Fairbridge Society, all of which admit ruefully the policy would never exist today and emphasise their commitment to helping any children involved to find out about their natural parents and backgrounds.

... of these children came to ... ago when a ...

... children's home in Britain and I learnt a lot of children had been sent postwar.

"I had known children went to Canada before the war but I was not aware they had left this country in the '50s in migration schemes." More than 3000 were sent between 1947 and 1951.

The idea seemed amazing and she was slightly incredulous. "I just wondered if it was absolutely accurate because she went out at such a young age, six. I could not comprehend how she had not been adopted or fostered."

That child was Mary, now a 38-year-old nurse, who had spent her life feeling bitter and confused about her past and convinced she had done something wrong to be "transported" to Australia.

Following the discovery of the postwar ... scheme, an advertisement ... Australian newspapers ... who had ...

... in a foreign, and what some ... hostile, environment. Stori... plain living conditions ... bleached calico clothe... mince for meals ever... abuse.

Now a trust has ... any of the adult... Australia with ch... to discover their ...

One of the ... in the Notti... ment of ... Social We...

"It's ... really ... think ... just ...

True survivor looks back on nightmare existence

By ROBYN CHALKLEN

ON A boat bound for Western Australia, a young English boy waited excitedly for a new life of adventure, good food and love.

His dreams were shattered when he arrived at Bindoon, a boys' home run by a Catholic order brothers instead of nuns.

He had escaped from one strict and cruel orphanage into another — a living hell he was to suffer for four years until he escaped at 16.

His name is Lionel Welsh, Geo...

"Kids of nine were building huge structures hacked out of virgin scrub"

Brought up and educated by nuns in England, he thought the trip to Australia was the dream of a lifetime.

"But it was a cruel trick — kids of ... were buil...

... where I had been for the past 10 days — all I knew was that I had to get something to drink.

"I thought about killing myself but the training at Bindoon had been good for one thing — they said the hell I would face would be worse than the hell I was living in."

Withdrawal

He eventually turned to Alcoholics Anonymous and many ...

The nightmare at Bindoon

THE first Bindoon migrants. This picture was taken in 1947.

A tyrant who taught loyalty

WHATEVER dark deeds may have occurred there in the past, the old Bindoon Boys' Town is the site of an excellent agricultural college bearing the name of the man who cast such a large shadow over Nigel Fitzgibbon and his friends.

The man from whom it gets its name, Brother Paul Francis Keaney, was born in Ireland in 1888 and migrated to Australia in 1911. He died at Bindoon in 1965.

But even his critics, such as Fitzgibbon, give him credit for instilling in the boys the need to learn a trade and for displaying loyalty to ex-Bindoon boys.

● Brother Keaney

THE small, slightly-built boy thought his luck was changing when the nuns in the Welsh orphanage told him he would be going to Australia.

It was April, 1947. Nigel Fitzgibbon was 13 and had not seen his parents for 10 years.

His mother had registered him in her maiden name to reduce the chances of her husband being able to trace the boy. Then she took a train to London and was never heard from again.

Now, with the excitement of medical checks, travel documents and new clothes for the voyage to Fremantle, Nigel's hopes for a better life looked like coming true.

On August 15, the 30 boys arrived at Southampton and boarded the liner SS Asturias with about 1000 other passengers. Of these, about 250 were boys and girls destined for other church-run farm schools and orphanages in WA.

The rest of the passenger list was made up of assisted-passage migrants and displaced persons, mainly Polish soldiers.

"Life on the ship was good," Mr Fitzgibbon recalls. "The food was the best I'd had and there were games and activities."

The best part for the youngsters was a pet monkey owned by one of the Polish soldiers. They watched entranced as it performed somersaults, smoked cigarettes and pilfered from the pockets of unsuspecting bystanders.

"As we approached Fremantle the ship's skipper, Captain J. Carr, offered two pounds to the first orphan to sight the coast of Australia, a prize which went to a young Welsh boy, John Coniffe.

"The Astaurius entered the port with the radios blaring out stirring martial music and *Advance Australia Fair*."

By ANDRE MALAN

Once ashore they were fingerprinted and the Catholics were assembled for a blessing from Archbishop Redmond Prendiville.

Soon after there were tears when the children heard that the Polish soldier's monkey had been killed by quarantine officials.

From the docks they were taken to the Clontarf orphanage south of Perth for a welcoming reception. Two hours later, Nigel Fitzgibbon and his friends were on their way to Boys' Town at Bindoon, 95km away.

Mr Fitzgibbon is now 53 and still lives in WA. He describes the three years he spent at Bindoon from 1947 to 1950 as a nightmare.

A NORMALLY genial man, he speaks angrily and with passion about the ill-treatment, sexual abuse and overwork he and the others were subjected to — treatment which, he says, caused psychological scars from which many ex-Boys' Town residents still suffer.

No serious attempt was ever made to educate the new arrivals and discipline gradually increased, the boys receiving frequent beltings with leather harness straps.

In February 1948 the boys heard with concern of the return to Bindoon of Brother Paul Keaney, who had lived there once before and had a reputation as an iron disciplinarian and fierce taskmaster.

Keaney set about building three large stone and granite buildings.

Mr Fitzgibbon recalls: "It was sheer slave labour with primitive tools from dawn to late evening. Visitors were always impressed by Keaney's zeal and passion for getting the work done but never realised the terrible cost to the boys.

"We had cement burns on our hands and feet and our bodies were nearly emaciated.

"We had no decent clothing and there were never any outings or other recreation.

"My first contact with Brother Keaney was devastating. One day when I was 13 he called me up to him and asked me what I wanted to be. I said I didn't know and without warning his huge first slammed into my face, breaking my nose and knocking me down.

"That night, for the first and only time, I cried in my bed and asked 'Where's my dad?'

"Two years later I and another boy named Bernard Binns had almost completed the granite structure for the big statue of Christ the King — the Prince of Peace, when Keaney came through the bush, shouting, swearing and abusing us. We were both whacked about the body with a huge stick. Bernard Binns flew off through the bush and I never saw him again."

Five days after the young Fitzgibbon arrived he was confined to bed by an insect bite which made his face swell alarmingly.

That evening an elderly brother came into the dormitory and tried to fondle him under the bedclothes.

"I was terrified and didn't know what to do. Fortunately one of the other boys came in to visit me just then and the brother walked away," he said.

"Brother Keaney had a disturbing habit of punishing boys by making them stand on a table and drop their trousers. He'd then call out 'Lift your curtain Biddy Ann,' a signal for them to raise their shirts so they could be belted on their bare backsides."

But there was revenge of a sort, Mr Fitzgibbon recalls. "We used to trap as many rabbits as we could to save the expense of meat.

"There were many feral cats on the property and often these cats got caught in our traps.

"The Spanish Benedictine nuns used to cook for the brothers and an old Aboriginal woman cooked for the boys.

"I must admit I made sure the carcasses of any cats I caught in my traps were included with the rabbits Sisters Hildegaard and Francis kept aside for the dining table of the brothers."

26 The Western Mail Weekend, August 15-16, 1987

II

Geordie
Orphan of the Empire

L. P. WELSH

P&B PRESS
Perth, Australia.

First published privately 1988
This revised edition published 1990
by:

P & B PRESS
P.O. Box 81
COMO WA 6152
AUSTRALIA

I.S.B.N. 0 9596606 5 8

Photograph on cover by Brian Marchant, Adelaide.
Typesetting by Caxtons, 10 Golding Street, West Perth, Western Australia.

To my fellow sufferers in Boys Town, Bindoon, Western Australia. Also to my friends on Skid Row who died that I might live and tell this story, and to our women who suffered for and with us.

I thank members of Alcoholics Anonymous everywhere, but especially those in Newcastle and Sydney, N.S.W. I also thank those close friends without whose love and tolerance, the writing of this story would have been impossible.

For years you watched me slowly dying,
Gave your love, helped stop me crying.
Because of this, today I can
Be the man you know I am.

During the first sixteen years of my life, I was known as Spoug. How I got that name, I will never know.

During my drinking heyday, I was called Geordie, because people born around Newcastle-on-Tyne are known as Geordies.

CONTENTS

INTRODUCTION

There will be those who condemn me and who will disbelieve this account of my first sixteen years. Some will cry, "Why resurrect the past? Why sully the names of people long since dead?"

I respond by saying that the truth cannot and should not be suppressed.

While many of the tyrants involved are dead, we who are left live with the scars of those nightmare years – the twisted concepts of religion, sex, authority, morality, relationships and all things related to a normal life. At fifty four, I struggle with these same scars which make it difficult for me to establish a normal relationship. So many have been smashed because of character defects formed in my early childhood. Alcohol did not cause these defects. It just allowed me to live with them.

I have despaired many times at my seemingly hopeless attempts to live a normal life. It is an ongoing struggle and I pray that one day, God, in His mercy, will extract by the roots the legacy those people have left me; that one day, somehow, my friends and I may be able to find a measure of security, contentment and peace.

I did not write this book to attack or defame anyone, living or dead. It is not meant to be an indictment of the Catholic Church or its adherents. I know that there were victims incarcerated in orphanages conducted by other religions and organizations who probably suffered as much as my friends and I. But I had to write the truth and this story records the truth as it happened to me. I wrote it, hoping it may give hope to those who have experienced, or are experiencing similar adversities.

I know it is hard to believe. Had it not happened to me, I too, would probably be one who may doubt and condemn the author's motives.

CHAPTER

1

From childhood hour I have not been
As others were – I have not been
As others saw – I could not bring
My passions from another Spring
..... And all I loved – I loved alone.
Edgar Allan Poe

I was born in Newcastle-upon Tyne, England, three years prior to the Second World War.

Until I was fifteen years of age, I knew nothing of my parents. Parting when I was two, they placed my sister Maureen and me in a Catholic orphanage where I was to spend the next ten years. Maureen was transferred to another orphanage two years later and we were not to see each other for more than twenty years.

These were years when the Church ruled with a rod of iron. Fear of the Papacy, eternal damnation in the flames of hell or a couple of thousand years in purgatory were its weapons. In the North East Boys Home, this terrible fear was to be drilled into me every day for the next eight years – morning, noon and night. It was to develop in me twisted concepts of all things, Christian and moral.

I have few recollections of the early years of my life, but there are some incidents I shall never forget as long as I live. Those people were well trained in every aspect of mental cruelty reinforced with religious indoctrination. From as early as I can remember, prayers were recited three times daily to God, the Virgin Mary or whoever else took their fancy. Mass was a daily thing, recited in Latin, none of which I understood. Going to Church and praying was something that had to be done, like using one's bowels or having a meal.

After Mass would come breakfast which, except on Sunday, was always porridge. Sunday breakfast was a meal to look forward to. It was the meal of the week, entirely different. It consisted of black pudding, sausages and probably horse meat and gravy. Also, on each table was a jug of tea. The tea was special as cocoa was the everyday drink. But Sunday breakfast was, for me, a time of fear and apprehension. I was always concerned about the bigger boys at the table. They stole my Sunday breakfast, drank all the tea and I was helpless. Should I want my fair share, I would have to fight the biggest bully at the table. That was the code. I hadn't learned to fight, so I always went hungry.

Sunday should have been a good day, but it never was. I had been to Mass and said my prayers. If Jesus was a kind man, why did He let this happen? And every Sunday! It didn't add up.

But Easter Sunday made up for them all. This day was talked about a month before it arrived. It was the day we got our one egg of the year. Nobody took it from you or even touched it. That was taboo. I can remember lying in bed the night before Easter Sunday and praying to God, "Please God, don't let me die tonight. Not before I get my egg." He must have been a good God as I always got my egg.

Perhaps, because of the war years, our diet consisted mainly of fish and potatoes. There were many times I got sick of eating this mess but only tried once to leave it uneaten. I just sat there and looked at it, and it was obvious to Sister that I had no intention of eating it.

She just said, "You don't want it?"

I shook my head and she took the meal off the table and placed it in the cupboard. I wondered why she put it in there. Next meal time came around and the same meal of fish and potatoes was placed in front of me. It had dried out and smelt horrible. I looked at it and still refused to eat it. At the end of meal, Sister came along and put the mess back in the cupboard. Then I began to worry. What is she doing? A third time the mess was put in front of me – with a glass of water placed beside the plate. The nun then stood behind me, took my nose in a firm grip and tilted my head back. She then picked up a spoonful of this putrid mess, shoved it in my mouth and picking up the glass of water, poured some of it on top of the food. It forced me to swallow or choke and, at the same time I wanted to vomit. The whole meal was disposed of in this manner. I wanted to throw it up but was frightened of the consequences. My little friends could only watch with pity in their eyes. All of us always ate all of our meals after that cruel demonstration.

Another method of punishment which terrified us was the bath treatment. In the cold climate of England we bathed once a week – on Saturdays. The bath water would have plenty of strong disinfectant in it. Should I have misbehaved during the week, quite often nothing was said and I would think Sister had forgotten.

Then, when I was in the bath, she would quietly say, "Do you remember so-and-so?"

Fear would grip me and I knew what was coming. She took me by the back of the head and pushed it under the water. Panic stricken, I would struggle, try to scream and, of course, get a mouth full and a nose full of filthy water and this would continue until I ceased to struggle. This type of treatment filled me with hate and rebellion. It was wrong and I knew it, but I was only six years old and couldn't work out why.

At least I had the consolation of my little friends. It is strange how pain and suffering form a strong bond. I could always be assured of a kind word or a little hug from one of the other boys. I guess, without knowing, we were becoming a close-knit family. Well, we were all brothers in the same boat.

Some of the boys had relatives, even parents, who would come and visit them from time to time – a happy occasion until the time of parting, then very sad. For me it was always difficult. Where did I come from? Don't I have anybody? I had been told by the Nuns that I had been found outside the Convent door in a blanket and I had to believe it. But once, just once I can remember when two ladies came to see me and, for some reason, I started to cry. This irritated the Nun and I thought, "She doesn't like this. Here's a chance to get even" so I cried louder.

She hit me and that made it worse. I cried louder and made up my mind, "The more you hit me, the louder I will scream. And I don't care how hard you hit me, I won't stop." It was not long before I was screaming my head off and loving it! By this time the Nun was furious.

She picked me up around the waist, swung me over her hip and made for the stone steps down to the cellar where the furnaces were. I stopped crying and, knowing where we were going, my crying became moans of fear. We got to the small, dirty brown door and she knocked. The little man who tended the furnaces opened it. Still on the Nun's hip, we went into a long, dimly lit tunnel. It was hot in there and I was petrified. Up to this point, the Nun had not said a word.

Then she whispered, "This is where little boys go who don't stop crying".

She told the little man to lift up the cover of a huge manhole in the tunnel floor. The cover was lifted off the manhole. It was a cleaning hole for the furnace flues. And, still on the Nun's hip, petrified, I was looking down into the hole, full of black smoke and flames. With me still on her hip, she went down on one knee to bring my head level with the top of the manhole. The fear was so great I couldn't even scream. I thought, "She's going to drop me in there!"

She told me it was Hell! I must have passed out – I do not remember anything else. But I do remember the nightmares and the awful vision of Hell which haunted me for years. God was kind! How can He do this? He was becoming a cruel old man or these people were lying to me about Him. But why?

The Nuns also taught us at school and here I must give them full marks. I was soon to learn that I had a sharp brain, and I always topped the class, especially in maths and handwriting. I was often entered in handwriting competitions outside the orphanage, though I never heard the outcome of any of the entries. I loved school. Perhaps it was a rest from the continuous torment that always troubled my mind. My brain would never stop. I was always worried about fearful things and always asking why.

But there were respites from the constant fear. We played the games other children played with the few toys we had and, of course, those we invented. In winter, we skated on the ice in boots or bare feet. It didn't matter. In summer, we played cricket and in winter, soccer. We stole the apples off the trees, chased the cows, looked for birds' nests and that aspect was, I suppose, the most normal part of our daily lives.

There were more than one hundred boys in the orphanage from all over the British Isles. I loved my friends and fought my enemies. And of course, being children, we were always hungry. I can remember one day I found some charred bones in the pig bin and had a feast on them in a hiding place.

This hunger was a little too much for Charlie and me. One day, at the peril of our lives, we robbed the Church poor box and thought we had got away with it. The haul netted 1/6d. We were rich! We ran as fast as we could to the store, bought five cigs, a jar of jam and some bread. Then we made for the hay loft and stuffed ourselves with bread and jam. Lying back in the hay and choking on Woodbines like two professional hoods, we talked of the success and daring of the job. We then made our way back to the play yard.

It was not long before we were called inside. I was scared. I knew that to steal from the poor-box in the Church was a terrible crime and that the punishment would be bad. I wasn't wrong. First, the flogging with the cane, then, for the next two or three hours I had to kneel erect on the cold concrete floor and go without lunch. After this, I was made to scrub a concrete passage about thirty feet long on my hands and knees and was then sent to bed without tea. We thought we had got away with it but, the Priest had seen the whole thing.

I was nine years old and this was the age we were allocated jobs of work, such as scrubbing floors, peeling potatoes and working in the kitchen, darning holes in our socks and sewing our numbers into them. Just like a prison, we all had identification numbers which were used more often than one's name. In springtime, we would rake and cart the hay, dig the potatoes and help to spread the manure over the fields. These and many other tasks we had to perform, always praying to the Saints to help us. They never did. Well, I didn't ever see any of them helping!

We always had to wash up after meals. I dreaded this. It meant going down into the cellar where the washing up was done. I was frightened to go down there. It stank. There were rats down there but worst and most frightening of all were the cockroaches. The dirty sink was always infested with them, so thick I could hear them moving. My skin would crawl and I would want to vomit and run, but I dare not. If I did I would be belted and humiliated. The humiliation always hurt more than the stick and I would muster the courage to somehow get the cockroaches out of the sink and wash the dishes. On occasions such as this, I would pray to Mary and the Saints, but they never came.

I was about ten years old when I was given the task of cleaning out a blocked toilet. It was full to the brim of turds – all shapes and sizes and various colours and they all stank. I looked at it and smelt it and started to retch, knowing the only way I could clear it was with my hands and a tin. I cleaned out as much as I could with the tin and the remainder with my hands. I do not have the words to describe it, but it was better than being humiliated.

These were the years of the second world war and this added more fear, especially at night. We could hear the planes flying over, the bombs exploding and, worst of all, the air raid sirens. The noise in the middle of the night, in the pitch dark, was frightening. When the siren went, we had to get out of bed, grab a blanket and, with the Nun in front holding a candle, follow her down the cold, concrete steps to the basement where we would lie on the floor and listen to the noises around us.

As if this was not enough, the Nun would start, "I hope you have been good and haven't committed any mortal sins. If you have and you are killed by a bomb tonight, then you will go to hell for ever. If you have any venial sins on your soul, you will have to burn in purgatory until your soul is as white as snow."

Then we would have to say the Rosary. I could not even think straight, let alone pray. I was just scared. I do not know how long these raids lasted, but they were always for ever.

However, there were some pleasant moments. I worked a lot in the kitchen where Mary and Joan worked. Mary was nice and very pretty and, at the age of ten, I was in love with her. She had lovely eyes and I loved the way her shirt would stick out at the front. But I loved it most of all when she would get down to scrub the floors. She would tuck her dress into the leg of her knickers and when she was kneeling down I could see right up to the crotch of her pants. This always excited me but I didn't know why. At times, I would have to scrub the floors – I loved it. This gave me a chance to look up her dress and I would always offer to do that job.

There was a peephole in the Nun's cubicle, which was exciting. I always wondered if they had any hair on their heads and what a Saint looked like under all that cloth. I was very curious. The Nun's cubicle was in the corner of the dormitory. We called it the cell. One night, curiosity got the better of me and I had to find out. Sister always came in after we had all been put to bed and so I waited. She came in, went into her cell and turned the light on as always.

I crept over to her cell, shaking with excitement. If I got caught, I would be flogged to within an inch of my life and I knew this, but it didn't matter. I peeped through the hole. She was just taking off the thing on her head. Yes, she had hair, though cut very short and she had ears, too. Her face was lovely. She would have been about nineteen years old. She then slipped the top of her habit down to her waist and for the first time in my life I saw a woman's breasts, though I did not know what they were; they were lovely. She then slipped her nightie over her head and in one movement, drew it down to her waist, while in the same movement pushing her habit down, covering the lower half of her body as she went. Very disappointed, I was left wondering, for many years, what was under the habit from the waist down. I went back to bed. I have forgotten what was going through my mind at the time, but I had at least seen the Sister Mary with no clothes on. That was a victory...and I didn't get caught.

That was one dormitory. There were two of them. Sister Ignatius slept in the cell of the other one. I was frightened of her, but I had to know what she looked like under her habit. The chance came.

By this time I had become an altar boy and at times had to be up at five o'clock to serve on Father at Holy Mass. Sister Ignatius had to wake me. She did this and then went back to bed. It was still very dark. I went into the other room to put on my altar boy's clothes and thought, "Sister Ignatius will be getting up now".

I knew what I was going to do and started to shake for the same reasons as before, although this time my fear was much greater. I looked through the peephole. She was just getting out of bed. Shit, she had hair too, but it was long and black with some grey mixed in. She was about forty years old. Next, she sat on the chamber pot and had a leak. She put a piece of cloth around the top to deaden the noise. Then, the same as Sister Mary, she slipped her nightie down to her waist. What a sight! Her tits were huge and I really started to shake. I bolted while the going was good. I was scared of being caught. Shit! I'd be as good as dead! But it was worth it. I had dared to break the rules. I had looked at a Saint half naked – that was contrary to all I had been taught – as bad as looking at the Virgin Mary half naked! How could I tell the Priest this at confession? But I was happy I had seen them in that state and, as far as I knew, they did not know I knew about it. And, even if they did, I had won. In my mind, I had stripped something away from them, though I did not know what. I never did that again; there was no need to. But for ages, I dreaded bath time. If they knew, I was sure they would have drowned me.

Although I had had about eight years of good Catholic upbringing, here I was, dressed as an altar boy ready to assist the Priest perform the most sacred ritual in Catholicism, perving on a nun's tits and her having a leak. Something was amiss, but what? Hadn't I been baptized, received Holy Communion, been confirmed, sprinkled many times with holy water, blessed by Mary and the Saints on many occasions, gone to Mass every day, rosary at night, had the fear of Hell and the Devil hammered into me every day? Yet here I was doing something not even the Pope could get me out of. It was confusing and did not add up. It left me feeling insecure. But this very victory over the naked Nuns left me with a perverted sense of ego. I had exposed something about them to myself and sensed a weakness in them. I felt as though I had a slight edge on them – just enough to try them out again. And I did!

This time, it was the biggest sin I could commit as far as

I knew then. I had a beautiful soprano voice and sang solo on special occasions such as Christmas and Easter. Sister Ignatius had been giving me a hard time at music lessons and I wanted to get even. She was very proud of her pupil's singing and I loved to sing solo. Sometimes I would have loved to have sung a few notes out of tune, but I could never bring myself to do it – the harmony was too beautiful and I could not destroy it. I would do something worse that would really hurt her, something once again at the peril of my life and total damnation in the flames of Hell.

Holy Communion time came, straight after I had sung. Sister Ignatius was beaming with joy. Her pupil had given a great performance. She would be feeling very proud of me and herself. But I had not forgotten the pain she had put me through to perform that beautiful piece.

In those days of Catholic teaching, it was sacrilege for anyone but the Priest to touch the bread – the body of Christ – or in any way show desecration towards it. It was placed in the mouth by the Priest and there it stayed. This had been drilled into me for years and had instilled so much fear into me that to contradict these teachings, in any way, meant absolute disaster. But she had hurt me. I was going to hurt her.

After receiving Holy Communion, I went back to my seat and spat it out on top of the pew. Then I went and told Ignatius. Sister coughed. She went white and started to shake. She was horrified and I knew it.

She stammered, "Show me". I took her over to my pew. Immediately she cleared the area of other boys. I had to stay next to the bread. "Go and get Father", she said to one of the boys, "and tell him what's happened. Quickly!" She then looked down on me. "You did this on purpose, didn't you?" I knew that she knew and I didn't say a word. She was scared. This had never happened before and she was lost. I was also scared but my joy of having frightened her made up for it, even though I knew what I was going to get.

Along came Father in the robes especially meant for the occasion, with an altar boy on either side, each holding a lighted candle. The trio looked suitably solemn. I stood there, scared but amused. Ignatius stood beside me, head bent, white as a ghost and a look that said, "We are all doomed." The Priest looked at me as though I was Satan himself. I bowed my head in the contrite manner a good Catholic altar boy had been taught. Father blessed the bread, mumbled something in Latin, then lifted the bread off the pew and stuck it back in my mouth. I swallowed it. Ignatius gave a great sigh of relief. Father once again blessed the pew, me and Ignatius. Then he and the boys went on their way.

Of course, I was given a horrible beating with the leg of a chair and locked in the dormitory all day with no lunch or tea. But it was worth it. I had made a fool of Sister Ignatius and I was a hero for a long time. Nobody had pulled that stunt before and nobody ever did again. Not there anyway. Of course, I had to go to confession immediately in case I died before Friday night – the usual confession time.

Time went by, mostly in its mundane way. Mass in the morning, a porridge breakfast, fish and potatoes for lunch and tea, evening prayers and quite often a reminder of the ghosts, boogie men, hell and the Devil. So many times I lay in my bed, stiff with terror and when sleep did come, it was full of nightmares. Many times I was frightened to go to sleep. Prayers were useless, or maybe I was saying them wrong.

Then along came Mr Matthews, a real bastard. He must have been trained in the same school as the Nuns. Like the Nuns, he was a good maths teacher and well versed in cruelty. His favourite pastime was to torment us with his belt. It was a wide, heavy black belt which he wore around his waist. He would wrap it around his hand and flick it like a whip. Sometimes he would strike and purposely miss, just to taunt us. At other times he would make a strike, generally around the face, neck or legs and it really stung. He would also use it to herd us together like cattle, always flicking it, a sickly grin on his face. Like all these people, he was cruel and to be feared.

And there was Captain Pope – ex-British Army. He, as I now know, was a homosexual. He was never unkind and he seemed to take a great interest in three of the boys – three brothers. He often had one of them sitting on his knee, stroking the boy's leg very close to the 'private parts' and I thought it odd. But I did not know why. Then, one day, he had one of these boys standing on the table and, in the open, had his hand up the leg of his pants, stroking his penis. To complicate it more, the Nun walked in and he just carried on, playing with the boy in the same manner.

I expected the Nun to say or do something, but she didn't. Why? I knew what he was doing was dirty. We had been taught not to play with our own 'dicks', let alone with anybody else's. We would go to hell for that and so would anybody else who did the same thing. Why didn't she do or say something? They had been belting that stuff into me for years...what was going on?

I had been taught that the Pope and Jesus were kind and gentle but these people were not kind and gentle – they were the opposite. They were screwing me up and making a good job of it. My intelligence told me that their Christian principles did not add up to the correct answer.

Many years later, I was to discover why they were screwing me up. I liked school, especially maths. I would be given a problem and, with simple logic, would come up with the answer. At school I discovered I was not a dunce. I could work out the things that were put before me and always topped the class. And, best of all, school gave my mind the rest it needed from the torment of the problems I could not work out. I could not work out the Nuns at that time because of hidden factors I did not know about.

The confusion came from the fact that while these people were lifting me up academically, psychologically they were putting me down. Up..down..up..down. It was a see-saw that I could not get off because I could not see it at the time. Even though I see it now, I still do not see why they were so cruel. Why would they use fear and pain when Mary did not use it?

Today, I can pray for those people and not judge them any more when I recall the words of the Master: "If you hurt one of my children, it is better that a millstone be hung around your neck and you be cast into the sea." This applies to me; it is a pity the Nuns did not think it applied to them.

Eventually, I discovered my real age. I was ten years old. I was a 'big' boy now – I must have weighed five and half stone, wringing wet. I was to go out to a secondary school, St. Patrick's, which was about a mile away. I cannot express the joy this news brought me. For eight years I had watched the older 'big' boys walk down the road to the outside school and I longed for the day when it would be my turn to go and see what was out there. It was going to another planet, really it was. I was bursting with excitement. That night in bed, I prayed, "Please God, don't let me die tonight."

I lay there, frightened to go to sleep, just in case I had done something bad and this was the way He would punish me – instead of going out to school, I would die and go to Hell. "Dear God, I don't mind going to Hell tomorrow night – for ever, if you like – but, dear God, not tonight." And I probably prayed to Mary, Joseph and every Saint I knew – and a few I didn't – not forgetting the Pope, of course. I probably put him first. After all, he is God's representative on this earth. If anybody could get to God, it would have to be him. Yes, he was the one to talk to. I must have been talking to the right one, for I fell asleep.

The long awaited day came. Scrubbed up and wearing new clothes and boots, I took my first steps down that magic road to a world I had never seen before. For eight years, I had been locked up in the orphanage and knew nothing of the outside world. It was a strange mixture of feelings.

St. Pats was like any other school, I suppose, but to me it was an adventure and a challenge. I had always topped my class at the orphanage. But this was different. These kids were different. Some were Protestants. What were they like? We were always taught that they were different, to be feared, not to be spoken to and we dare not listen to anything they had to say about religion. They were our deadly enemies, not to be trusted at all. They persecuted the Catholics.

Were the Protestants brainier than us? No, they could not be. They did not even believe in the Pope or the Saints or Mary or anything. They must be dumb. Maybe they were cruel, but that would be O.K., I could handle that – I could fight. I had been taught by experts.

I entered that school with anxiety and fear. And you know what? Those kids in that school were no different to me! They didn't care where I came from and they were just as scared as

I was! It did not take long to make friends. And to make things better, there were girls there too. I had not seen any girls before – only Mary and Joan – but these were different. They were our age and some of them were beautiful. A couple of them did something to me inside, but I did not know what. They just stirred me up and I liked it.

Yes, I was going to like this school. It had a nice comfortable feeling about it. The teachers were strict, but certainly not as strict as the Nuns. They taught us well in maths, French, algebra, history and geometry. Except for the three Rs, the subjects were all new to me. I liked them all, except French.

The 'outside kids' as we called them, were good to me. They knew where I had come from and of course, as kids will, they felt sorry for me. One boy I befriended, McDermott, was a real character. He came from a poor home but always shared his lunch with me and I loved the ginger biscuits his mother made, but, at the same time, it made me sad.

The questions would start in my head: why did he have a mum and dad and I didn't and where did I come from? McDermott told me that everyone has a mum and dad and the other kids told me the same. Nobody gets born in a blanket outside a door. They said maybe my folks had been killed in the bombing, but I was dumped there in 1938, well before the war started.

McDermott came up with a possible answer. "Maybe you did get borned in a blanket – some kids might – I'll ask Ma tonight."

McDermott asked his mother. "No! Kids don't get born in blankets. They all have a mum and a dad. Dad puts something into Mum and that's how babies are made."

That is what my friend told me and I knew he was telling the truth. It made sense. But somebody had lied to me. One day I would find the answer. If they had told me one lie, maybe they had told me a lot more. These boys and girls were stirring something up in me. I was sure it was not envy or jealousy. Rather, it was a sad, forlorn feeling that I had to carry. I could not get the answers.

It did not take me long to settle into the routine of St. Pats. For a while the thought of going back to the orphanage after being away all day took a bit of getting used to. But one can get used to anything in time. I found the boys and girls were no different to us at all. They did not care what we believed in or where we came from. They, like us, just wanted to be pals. Why had the nuns told me they were bad people, not to be trusted? I could not work it out.

All of us boys did the same things – smoked behind the toilets, threw rocks at old ladies' doors, pinched their milk, teased the tramps, looked up the girls' dresses to see their knickers and all the other things kids do. We even fought the snotty-nosed kids from the Grammar School. We all stuck up for each other. Once again, confusion. Where was the difference? It rattled around in my head for a long time.

One of the boy's mothers from St Pats arranged for six of us to go to her house on a Saturday afternoon for a party. What a day to look forward to! I had never been in an outside house before. What would it be like? What did they do? What would I have to do? I was excited but nervous. The Nuns had told us to be on our best behaviour and to speak only when spoken to and not to forget our manners. I did not know what to expect. I supposed it would be the same routine as the orphanage because that was all I knew.

What a shock I got! There were four or five couples there and I had never seen or dreamed of anything like it. It was like a beautiful dream – the whole thing. People did not behave like this without wanting something. But these people did not want anything; they only wanted to give and make us happy. They had to be screwballs...I really mean that! As soon as we arrived, one of the ladies picked me up in her arms and kissed me and hugged me and then passed me on to the next one. The men patted my head and I knew they meant it. It was all very strange.

We were taken into the dining room and I could not believe what I saw – a table of beautiful food! That must be for them. I wondered where ours was. But this was different – it was for everybody. I could not believe it. What strange people! They even played games with us and treated us the same as the other kids who were there. But all afternoon, in the back of my mind, I thought, "I have to go back to that dump. Why can't it always be like this?"

Going-back time came and my heart dropped. Heaven was over and the best afternoon I had spent in my life. The love that was shown to me by these people was nice but it hurt – really hurt by the time I got back.

I was down in the dumps for a long time after that afternoon. I had looked at a world I did not know existed. Did people outside act like that all the time, or was it for our benefit? Had they put on a special show for us? Allan, whose home it was, assured me on Monday that the only thing special about it was the food but, yes, they always ate the same as the grown-ups and they all loved each other. As much as I had enjoyed the party, it left me confused with my mind asking a lot more questions, the main one, of course, being, "What's wrong?" I lived one life-style and, for a brief moment got to look at another, at the absolute extreme from the one I knew. Where was the middle line or which one was right?

Once a year, workmen would come to clean out the gutters of the home. They would put their extension ladders up sixty feet. During the year, the bigger, stronger boys would throw balls up on the roof and, of course, they would be lost in the gutters. I had always wanted a ball, but the bullies always got them. Maybe this year, when the workmen threw the balls down from the top of the ladder, I would be big and quick enough to get one. But I was still very small and did not like my chances. Every year, we all waited at the bottom of the ladder, pushing for the best position, the big boys always winning. That year, I did not get a ball either, but when the men knocked off at night the ladder was still there. They had not finished and I knew what to do. This year I would get a ball – at any price. I would climb that ladder and get one.

After tea and being summer, there was still a little daylight left. I stood at the bottom of the ladder. It was a long way up and I was scared, but my determination to get a ball overcame my fear and slowly I started to climb. After what seemed a very long time, I reached the top, shaking like a leaf. My right hand felt along the gutter...no ball...my heart sank and I wanted to get down. There might be a ball on the other side. Carefully, I climbed down the ladder, my little legs hardly able to support me, they were shaking so much. In frustration, I started to cry.

A few days later, Sister told me that she had been standing at the window on the third floor and had seen me going up but was so frightened she did not dare say a word in case I fell. And strangely enough, I did not get the belting I thought I surely would.

About a month before Christmas, parcels would start arriving for boys with parents, to be opened on Christmas Day. The Nun would lock them up in a big cupboard in the playroom without a word to anybody. We would all stand there and watch her put them in, never knowing who they were for and, like all past years, I hoped maybe this year there would be one for me. By the time Christmas Day arrived, the cupboard would always be full. With all those parcels in there, there just had to be one for me.

Breakfast time on Christmas Day was always one of excitement and hope. As always, Sister would open the big cupboard straight after breakfast. The porridge was never eaten so quickly and then down to the playroom to wait at the cupboard for Sister. On this occasion, nobody ever pushed anybody around for the best position. We just stood there quietly, hoping. Sister would open the cupboard, take the parcels out one by one and call the names of the boy whose names was on it. Maybe the next one will be for me. The cupboard would be getting emptier and, like other years, my heart would begin to sink. I only want a little one, I don't care who from, just so I would not have to stand there and feel the hurt again. But, as always, there was no parcel for me and a couple of the other boys. The same few of us every year. We would just bow our heads, very hurt. The Sister, God bless her on this occasion, would show some compassion and give us some sweets. This happened every year and was one of the things I never got used to. Even to this day, I hate Christmas Day.

Then came the day to make the suffering of the past ten years all worthwhile.

"Who wants to go to Australia?"

Was I dreaming? Was this for real? It was now 1947. I had been locked in that place for nearly ten years. Here was a chance to get out. Or were they joking? They had to be. It was too good to be true. Siberia had to be better than this place. But Australia it was! Gee!

Nothing was said about it for a long time. Of course, I should have known – another of their jokes. Then, once again we were assembled and the lucky names called out. Mine was one of them! I could not believe it! Could this really be true? I was going to get out of jail! And going to Australia...twelve thousand miles away! It was a miracle!

From that night on, I prayed to everybody not to let me die before I went to Australia. Even if I just get there and die, I won't mind. Please just let me out of here. And it really was true! We were measured for clothes, given a heap of injections and, of course, told that in Australia we would ride horses to school, chase kangaroos and do things we had never dreamed of doing before.

What seemed like an eternity eventually ended. The day arrived for us to leave! Dressed in new clothes, scrubbed up and excited, we were assembled, given a last lecture by the Nuns and nearly drowned in the Holy Water sprinkled on us by the Priest who blessed us three or four times before departing.

"Cut out the bullshit", I thought, "and let's get out of here!"

It was early November, 1947. We were taken by train to Southampton where the S.S. "Asturias" was waiting to take us to the Land of Milk and Honey and freedom from the Tyrants.

Gone forever were the days of physical and mental cruelty. I could leave it all behind. This was the happiest day of my life! With the aid of the British Government and the Catholic Migration Authority, we set sail for Australia. It was the only time in my life I had seen the Nuns show any emotion. They must have had some humanity in them somewhere, but it was far too late for that. The damage had already been done. The fear, insecurity, twisted concepts and hate had been well sown and nurtured. The die had been cast.

Do you ever wonder why a gentle and intelligent person, whose kind, soft eyes have looked on you with love and cried with you in pain...how those same eyes, in an instant of rage, can turn black with insanity and hate? The gentle hands that caress your face can, in a moment, turn to claws of steel to choke you – and a beautiful, innocent child is made into a hardened criminal.

CHAPTER 2

> It were still wiser to say that behind sorrow
> there is always a soul.
> And to mock at a soul is a dreadful thing.
> Unbeautiful are their lives who do it.
> Oscar Wilde

We set sail for the 'Promised Land'.

The first couple of days I was seasick, but after that I was like a wild animal let out of a cage and, had it not been for the previous years of harsh training, would have gone berserk.

There were probably two or three hundred orphans on the ship from all over the British Isles – girls and boys from nine to sixteen years, all brought up in the same way. But we were not strangers for very long. We were like one big family with two old Nuns trying to look after us with the help of a few Catholic passengers.

Every night, the two Nuns would gather us in one of the dining rooms and say, "The ship will go down tonight if you don't behave and say your prayers."

It was water off a duck's back. None of the other passengers seemed to be worried, so why should I? Anyway, I was free and these two silly old Nuns were not going to spoil my freedom. I was becoming old enough to know they were bluffing. So I smoked, played with the girls and had the time of my life. Once again, I found that, although a lot of the people on the ship were not Catholic, they were no different to us and if anything, they were better than us. Certainly better than the Nuns. One couple took to me and told me they would adopt me when we got to Australia but of course, they never did.

One thing that amazed me was that we were treated the same as everybody else on board by the passengers and crew. Even in the dining room, we were given the same food. It was real food and we were waited on too! I could not understand it. We were being treated as human beings. Surely people did not live like this all the time. They seemed to be free, ate good food and nobody bossed them around. Maybe that's how people acted on ships, but not in real life. It was like living in a dream and I loved every minute of it.

All good things come to an end. The mainland of Australia had been sighted. We would land the next day. The party was over and it was then I started to think, "Where are we going? What sort of home? It couldn't be as bad as the one I had left – nothing could be as bad as that! Nobody could be as nasty as those people. Australian people would be different – they had to be; they lived in a different country."

On the 10th December, 1947, we landed at Fremantle in Western Australia. On leaving the ship, we were assembled into groups on the wharf. It was hot. Bloody hot! We were then put on buses and transported to a big hall where there were lots of nuns and priests and a couple of bishops. Somebody gave a speech, we were given a feed and then herded on to other buses to be taken to a place called Boys Town at Bindoon, sixty five miles from Perth.

Although it was only about a two hour journey, it seemed to take for ever. I looked out of the window and there, looking back at me were two massive stone pillars with a large sign spanning them. It read, "BOYS TOWN, BINDOON". I did not like the look of it.

We drove through the gates on to a gravel road in the middle of virgin bush, the like of which I had never seen before. Where were we going? After travelling about ten minutes, we rounded a corner and there, down in a small valley, was the new home I had travelled 12,000 miles for.

It looked beautiful. Two separate Spanish style stone buildings stood out against the red gravel. Another huge, unfinished stone structure lay to the side of the first two. Around about were scattered other smaller buildings of various material. The background to this was paddocks and bush. It looked beautiful but, at the same time, very forlorn and foreboding.

Originally, 17,000 acres had been donated to the Catholic Church by a Mrs Musk. The land was to be split into small farms for boys when they attained a certain age, and a little stock and some equipment was to be provided to help get them started. It was a kind and beautiful gesture. Then, about 1938, a Marist Brother – a Catholic of course – by the name of Francis Paul Keaney, was given or took on the task of getting this place off the ground. No doubt a formidable task, as the place was 65 miles from Perth and in virgin bush.

Keaney was quite a man – an Irishman who stood 6'2" and weighed 17 stone. He was loved, respected and known by anybody who was anybody in the Catholic Church from here to Timbuktu; from the Commissioner of Police to the most humble priest. He was known to be a hard, tough man and had a reputation for it. He gathered up the tough boys from institutions around Western Australia and took them to Bindoon where they set up tents by a waterhole called 'Bunji'. And in this harsh bush, with the help of an old Aboriginal cook called Rosie and a couple of other outsiders, he commenced to carve out a monument to himself. They had constructed the buildings I saw from the bus. One huge stone structure had been started. Who was going to finish it? It did not take me long to find out!

The bus moved slowly down the hill and as we approached the buildings, a lot of boys were there to meet us. They were also orphans who had been transported there from all over Britain. They were happy to see us. There were forty or fifty of them, all dressed in khaki shirts and shorts and, of course, we felt we had known them all our lives.

We got off the bus and were immediately herded into a big clothes room by one of the Brothers and I knew by the way he spoke – here it was again! My heart sank. Our kitbags and the nice clothes we wore were taken from us. We were given numbers – mine was 42. It was then I realized that I had walked into a situation exactly like the one I had left and I started to cry. The others must have felt the same; we were all crying.

The Nuns in England had told me, "You think we are hard. Wait till you meet the Christian Brothers. They are a lot harder than we are."

At the time I did not believe them. Nobody could be harder than them, just nobody! But it turned out the Nuns were only amateurs.

The crying became louder as we realized that we had been lied to yet again. We had been moved from one gaol to one much worse. How could they do this? How could they tell us we were going to a dreamland then dump us in the middle of the bush in a strange country with flies, mosquitoes, ants, poisonous snakes – all sorts of strange creatures – and to make things worse, the sun beating down at least '500 degrees'. I was fair skinned with blonde hair and had just left a country where it snowed and water sometimes froze in the pipes. Now the skin was burning off the soles of my feet, the sun was slowly cooking the rest of me and my new clothes had all been taken from me. And here I was, dumped in the middle of nowhere with a harder mob of tyrants than those I had left behind. The sun and other things were bad enough. I would get used to them, but I would never get used to the lie that I had been told, another one of many. That is what was really hurting. Why did they teach us not to lie, yet they did so openly themselves? Didn't they go to hell or any of the other places because they had been consecrated by a bishop?

And now, one of them, Brother McGee, the Principal Brother, was yelling out, "Stop your crying and whining or I'll give you a flogging. All of you!" This was my introduction to the Hell I was to remain in for the next four and a half years.

We settled down with the help of the boys who had already been there for a few months. The routine was the same as the one we had left. Rise at 6.30 a.m. and go straight to Mass, a breakfast of porridge, a slice of bread and an apology for a cup of tea. Straight after breakfast we went to our allocated jobs – to the dairy, piggery, fowl house, orchard, kitchen or whatever. On completion of the chores we went straight to school. Lunch at 12 noon – sheep flaps, cabbage and watery custard. Back to school at 1.00 p.m. and out at 3.30 and then straight to our chores till five o'clock. Showers at 5.30 – generally cold, winter and summer. Tea at six o'clock – either bread and milk or watery soup. Then straight to church for evening prayers for at least half an hour. One hour's play-time after church and then into bed and lights out at nine o'clock. The diet and the routine remained constant for the next four and a half years.

My job before and after school and on weekends was to milk two cows. Quite often, I had to go out to the paddock, winter and summer and herd the cows to the dairy. This job was cruel in winter as I had no shoes and had to walk through the frosty grass bare-footed. Often I would cry because my feet were so cold. It was on a morning such as this, when I was milking one of the cows, that she lifted her hoof and it came down on my foot. With her weight on my foot, she twisted her hoof and, in doing so, tore my big toe nail right off. My feet were freezing cold which was bad enough, but the pain of my toe was excruciating. I just put my head against her side and cried when the Brother in charge, Brother Dawe, saw me.

"What's wrong?" he asked.

Unable to speak, I pointed to my toe.

"Finish milking her" he said, "and I'll put something on it."

He did...it was iodine! I dared not scream. We had been trained not to do that. He was a cruel man and I learned to hate him with a terrible intensity.

Another time, this same man vented his sadism on me as he was to do many times. Again, it was a freezing cold morning and my friend, Joe Norman and I arrived at the dairy two minutes late. Brother Dawe, or Honk, as we called him, was waiting for us with an axe handle in his hand. I was filled with fear. Joe and I looked at each other and, quietly, in a trembling voice, Joe whispered, "He wouldn't use that, would he Spoug?"

I was fairly sure he would. I remembered the toe-nail. We reached him, freezing cold, our only protection from the weather thin shorts and shirts.

He looked at his watch. "You're two minutes late!" Turning to Joe, he said, "Bend over."

I could not believe it. These bastards were cruel, but no, not this cruel! It's freezing cold, you can't, nobody could do this!

Joe bent over. Honk brought the axe handle down on his backside with force. Joe whimpered. To cry out would be to invite another stroke. Then it was my turn. Terrified, I bent over, my legs shaking. The force of the blow jarred my buttocks and the searing pain made me want to vomit. The physical pain was bad, but nowhere near as bad as the knowledge that a powerful, grown man could do this to children much smaller than himself and absolutely defenceless against him. Where was God now? Why didn't He take the pain away?

The place was run by Brother McGee. He had the help of five or six other Brothers, Rosie the cook and three laymen they called 'staff'. They taught us how to look after the cows, fowls, pigs, horses, sheep, vineyards, orchards and all the other things associated with a farm. I liked this part of it. It was new and very different to the life in England. I was becoming used to the flies and heat and could always, in summer, cool off in the swimming pool which was formed from a damned up creek. We explored the bush, learned to trap rabbits and built cubby houses. At least this was different, even though the cruel treatment remained the same. And now, too, there was the Saturday night picture show to look forward to, as the Brothers had their own projectors and would obtain the films from Perth. The picture show always made up for the bad and sad events of the week and was a talking point. Things were not that bad, after all.

Something out of the ordinary was Old Don. I first noticed him one day as I was playing in a disused General Grant tank, a remnant of the war. Looking through the peephole of the tank, I saw this short but powerfully built man walking down the paddock towards me. He was crudely dressed and wore an old bashed-up army hat. As he got closer, I noticed he was talking to something on the ground and I assumed he had a small dog that I could not see at that distance. He kept coming and talking to the dog I thought he had, but as he passed me, I could clearly see that there was no dog or anything else in sight. I was puzzled and asked one of the older boys about him. He had come from a very wealthy family it seemed and had studied to be a doctor. The study became too much for him and his mind snapped. His family had sent him to Boys Town.

Then the news got around. Brother Keaney was coming back! We had been told of this man – the methods he had used to start the place off, where he had got the labour and that he was a really tough Irishman and intended to carry on building where he had left off. I did not think much about it. My body was hard and so was my mind. Things could not get much tougher. Probably all bullshit, anyway. He possibly wouldn't even come. But he did.

I will never forget the day he arrived. Yes, he was a giant and I, like all the other boys, was full of fear. He looked as tough as they said.

I was twelve years old, about 4'6" tall and probably weighed seven stone. Keaney towered over me. He was a strong man, known at one time to have lifted a young horse off its feet by getting between its legs and lifting with his shoulders.

A lot of people came that day. The Cream of the Catholic Church, he called them. They had good food to eat with plenty of booze and a lot of them got drunk. But of course, before the revelry, the usual prayers were said. Everybody was blessed by the Priest with the reverence only the Catholic Church can muster for such an occasion. When it was over, we cleaned up and ate the scraps and were made to feel privileged to be able to do so.

It did not take Keaney long to get started on the building project and pick up where he had left off a few years before. He brought in an old Italian bricklayer from the old days, Joe Pascoli. Joe was a good old fellow and we liked him. He was to teach us the art of laying bricks, plastering and everything that went with it. He was soon followed by a man called Gilpin to teach the skill of carpentry.

The Brothers knew nothing of the building trade and taught the skills of farming. Keaney's first project was a two-storied technical school, to be constructed of brick and stone, mostly stone. The property was strewn with it and there was plenty of cheap labour to gather it – boys from the age of nine to sixteen.

I was selected for the building gang. This entailed anything to do with cement or scaffolding. At the age of twelve, I was introduced to a pick and shovel, barefooted, and instructed in the art of digging a foundation in hard clay. I still had to milk my two cows before and after school and the time in between would be spent on the pick and shovel. It was hard and hot, the temperature at times over 100 degrees. But I soon toughened up to it – I had to.

Keaney was a hard man, though at times would show he had a good sense of humour. From the time he arrived at Boys Town, he indicated his dislike for the Saturday night picture shows which he considered a waste of time. I knew he would put a stop to them. He did and it did not take long. One morning at breakfast, he announced his watch had been stolen and that, until it was returned, there would be no more pictures. This was a terrible blow. We were to be deprived of the only real bit of pleasure we had. We knew none of us had the watch. It was taboo to do anything that everybody else would be punished for and pressure from everyone else would force the offender to own up. Instinct told us that none of us had it. Then where was his watch? We all came to the same conclusion – that he had lost it and was blaming us and that this was a trick to stop the pictures. They did stop – for nearly two years. Then one day a boy was digging the garden under Keaney's bedroom window and he dug up the missing watch. Rusty, it was given back to him. A couple of months later, we got our pictures back.

I knew what he had done. He had put it there himself. It was his puny excuse to stop our pictures. I thought, "One day I will out-smart you, you old bastard. You're like the rest of them – a fucking liar. You bastards are all the same. Probably all Christians are, too."

Keaney was obsessed by the building project. Apart from religion, it came second to nothing. The stone was gathered from the paddocks by us boys. We would load it onto a five ton truck, cart it to the site and there off-load it. There was no tip-tray. It was all done by hand. The sand was taken from a pit and hand-loaded on and off the truck. For small boys it was very hard work but we always had a Brother to supervise us. They were good at supervising! The gravel for concrete was handled in the same way as the sand – with the shovel. The material for the scaffolding, the poles and rails (known as standards and ledgers) was procured from the bush. Half a dozen of us would be piled on to the back of a truck and, with an axe each, taken out to the bush. We would select long, straight saplings, cut them down with the axe, trim the heads and strip the bark and load them on to the truck. The poles were lashed together with rope made from binder twine. We made the rope too.

All the boys took part in these activities, regardless of age and size. You picked up what you could carry, but you picked up something. The building took top priority over everything else, even over our education. It was standard practice for boys at school to be called out to carry ten bricks or stones each up to the older boys doing the work. They were past school age, which was then fourteen years. Or we spent an hour mixing mortar or concrete and then back to school.

School was a farce and I was very disappointed. The standard of education in Australia at that time was two to three years behind the standard in Britain. I am not knocking it – that is the way it was. I found I was being given work I had done two or three years before in England. It was very frustrating and I often thought, "What is going to happen to me? They're teaching me what I already know."

I was hungry for knowledge, especially in maths. Once again, I felt betrayed and often wished I was back with the Nuns who were not as hard as these people; where there was no work between lessons and, above all, where I could get the mental rest I needed from the fear and turmoil that was always inside my head.

To make matters worse, in the short time I spent at school in Western Australia, I must have had at least six different teachers with six different methods and who started at six different levels.

One tried to teach us bookkeeping. When he found we could not grasp it, he gave the whole thing away and would bring a pile of comics, put them on his table and say, "Read them." He would then lie back in his chair and, for the rest of the day, go to sleep. He was the bookkeeper for the place. In the middle of winter, freezing cold, he would, with just a towel around him, walk to the showers at 6.00 a.m. and under the shower, at the top of his voice, sing hymns and, of course, wake everybody up. We all thought he was a nut, and as it turned out, we were not wrong.

Another Brother was eighty years old. Keaney, no doubt

anxious to get our education over and done with, introduced this learned man to teach us advanced physics. It was ludicrous. None of us were ready for anything like that. He had brought all the text books and equipment for the job, but it was beyond us. Of course, we got the blame, were abused and told we were a pack of idiots and that put an end to the subject.

That is how our education went. I knew deep down that my chances of becoming an academic of any kind were gone. One could say that my schooling finished when I left Britain at the age of almost twelve. It was one of the most devastating blows meted out to me.

But not the most devastating. I will never forget the night Keaney asked me to sit in his office and wait for a trunk call from Perth that he was expecting, a job I often did. On this occasion, I went into the office and lying on the desk was a large blue-covered book and inscribed on the front cover, in gold letters, was the word "Registrations". Something clicked inside my head and with fear and apprehension, I timidly opened it. There, staring at me, were the names and details of my friends. Mine would be in here, too. I slowly went through the book until I found my name. And there it all was! The name and last known address of both my parents, my mother's maiden name, my date of birth. I could not believe it! I was stunned!

I had known over the years that they had lied to me on many occasions but here it was – the biggest lie, the biggest deceit. I was shocked.

But worse than that, unknown to me at that time, my mother had died of T.B. while I was incarcerated in Boys Town, Bindoon. The tears came to my eyes and I thought, "You bastards! Why have you done this? For so many years, all of us have asked you where we came from, where our parents were and you always silenced us with, 'We don't know.' Yet here is a book that denied everything you have told us."

I had learned to hate and despise these people, but this one piece of information intensified my hate and at that moment, I vowed that one day they would pay for it. How, I didn't know, but if ever I were given the opportunity, I would make them pay for the shocking lie they had not only told me, but to thousands of other children like me.

THE MOTHER I NEVER KNEW

It was a fellow recruit during National Service Training in 1955 who held the key to my past. An employee of the Child Welfare Department, he had access to my file and with his help, I discovered the whereabouts of my mother's family in England. Until then, all I knew about my origins had been gleaned from Keaney's book of registrations four years earlier.

Now, at last, I had a family and I was hungry for information. The painful questions and deep-seated longing which I had learned to cope with, were resurrected. Until I received this photograph from an aunt, I had no idea what my mother looked like. The accompanying letter set out the sad details.

My father left my mother when I was two years old and my sister six months. Mother supported us as best she could, scrubbing floors, washing, ironing and doing other menial chores.

The late thirties were hard times in the North of England, money was scarce and in winter, the temperature could drop below freezing. But Geordies are tough and she battled on for as long as she could.

She contracted T.B. and as, in those days, there was no cure, the time came when she had to make the painful but inevitable decision to let us go.

Her sisters were anxious to take us, but fate ruled otherwise. They were Protestants and as my mother had turned Catholic to marry, we were Catholic and our parents had agreed to rear us as such. The Church demanded this.

Our poor mother had no alternative than to hand us over to the care and custody of the Nuns at a nearby orphanage.

As a child, I was told that I had been found outside the orphanage in a blanket, an abandoned waif.

My mother died while I was at Boys Town, Bindoon. I was fifteen years of age. She died the same year I discovered her name in Keaney's impressive book of registrations.

The drudge continued. Prayers every day and night, out of the classroom, on to the building site, back to the classroom, a shocking diet, always in fear of a belting, the Devil, Hell, Ghosts and any other form of fear that could be used. Especially the strap; that was cruel. It was made of four or five pieces of leather, each about eighteen inches long and one inch cubed. It was a very formidable and painful instrument which the Brothers carried around in the hip pocket ready for any occasion they might see fit to use it. On many occasions, I was made to drop my shorts, bend over and have six of the best laid on my backside. To flinch meant an extra stroke. The pain of that strap was cruel, at times so painful I would want to vomit. We all dreaded it, but it was often used.

It was always used at Sunday School. No, not the Sunday School practised by other denominations – this was unique to Francis Paul Keaney. Every Sunday, he would assemble the Brothers in his office. We all knew why and we would discuss amongst ourselves who we thought would get it that day. I would be apprehensive, taking a look back at the week and asking myself if I had done anything to warrant the strap. Had I been seen in the lambing paddock or stealing grapes from the vineyard? Had I spoken too loudly? I was never sure and would wait the long hour. Then out Keaney would come and assemble us in the hall where he would place himself in a chair at the front, his little note book in hand.

"I hope my name's not in it."

Then, for effect, he would send one of the boys to his office to get his strap. I would sit there waiting, the palms of my hands sweating. The name of the offender would be called out.

He would walk to the front and stand before Keaney, trembling, and Keaney would then read out the complaint from the Brother who had been offended. He would then stand and order the boy to drop his shorts, bend over and lift his shirt tail up over his buttocks. Trembling and crying, the lad would do so. Taking the strap, Keaney would draw his arm back over his shoulder and, with brute force, swing it down and lay the strap across the naked buttocks. The tears would be running down the boy's face and he would be sobbing uncontrollably, but he dared not flinch or scream, lest he get an extra one for every time he did so. Inside, I would be crying for him. I felt his pain. I had been the victim on several occasions. The most hurtful aspect of it though, was to have to stand out there, completely on your own and be humiliated in front of all your mates.

Not satisfied with the flogging, Keaney would have to add further to the humilation with a remark like, "There's a few brains in the bottom storey, sonny, but the top storey's full of shit." Then he would call for the next offender. That is how we commenced the "Lord's Day".

The rest of Sunday we would spend in the bush, exploring and digging out rabbits, which we would clean and take to the kitchen from where they would be sent to 'Catholic friends' in Perth. The baby rabbits we would keep as pets and would carry one around inside our shirts. I had one and loved it. To feel its little, furry body inside my shirt – feel it running around in there – gave me a lovely feeling. I loved my little pet. Even though it was against the rules, we nearly all had one.

One day, happy with my little rabbit running around in my shirt, I was stopped by Honk. I froze.

"What have you got inside your shirt? Give it to me."

I handed over my tiny ball of fluff. He put its little neck between two fingers and, with a flick of his wrist, sent the little body through the air. The head of my pet was still in his hands. He threw it to me.

"Here's your pet."

Broken-hearted and crying, I walked away. I could not believe that anyone could be so cruel. Another coal to the fire of hate.

One day, somehow, somewhere, I will get square with you.

With the harsh life and treatment, there was always talk of running away. Some of the boys tried it but they were always brought back. Only one got away. It took tremendous courage to attempt 'bunking'. Two of my friends tried it – Jimmy Mecham and Tom Allan – and I witnessed another display of cruelty.

Terrified, the two of them were taken to Keaney's office. I was called off the building site to observe the punishment. He sensed I was going to try the same thing – I knew that was why I was there. Both boys were sobbing and trembling, for they knew the score. Keaney was in a rage. This man was to be feared at any time, but in this frame of mind he was capable of anything. I had seen him in his Irish temper before.

Inside, I was crying for my two friends. "Please God, help them. They are going to need it."

First, he hit them with a tirade of humiliating abuse and then he stood up and, armed with a strap, commenced to lash out at them. He flogged them around the whole of their bodies. They cried out for him to stop, but this only seemed to infuriate him more. With tears in my eyes, I began to walk out. I could not stand it. It was too cruel – the worst I had ever seen.

"Come back here! You will get worse if you try!"

I knew I would. He knew I was a smart boy and, if anyone could get away, it would be me. This was a warning. He gave the boys a few more lashes as I watched.

"If I ever try this" I thought, "you will never catch me. I will beat you for this, you fucking, cruel bastard."

Today, as I write, I re-live this scene. Had I not seen and experienced these things, I would never have dreamed human beings could be capable of meting out such cruel treatment to small children. It is difficult to write with an open mind.

I saw many displays of cruelty. Another concerned Jack Usher, Irish, sixteen years old and a very tough boy. He would raise his fists to Keaney, something unheard of, something none of us ever had the courage even to think about. But Jack did. He was tough and a real problem.

Jack's best friend was Peter Woods. Peter was liked by all of us. A good looking and quiet boy, he was slightly older than Jack, and left at sixteen, the age most boys left for the outside world.

Jack was really cut up on the day Peter left and he fretted for some time. One or two months later, word got back that Peter Woods was dead and his body would be brought back to be buried at Bindoon. Jack was devastated.

Peter's body was brought back to us four days later. It was the middle of summer and he stank. In his sleep, he had rolled off the back of a truck, his head and shoulders going under the dual wheels. His body was a mess. I had never seen death before and it terrified me. All of us were made to walk past the decomposing body of our friend whose brains were draining from his ears and his lovely face was contorted into an ugly shape. I saw this and it filled me with horror. I had many bad nights and nightmares for years after.

Of course, the Brothers capitalized on this, constantly reminding us not to worry if we saw Peter's ghost walking around or hear him start the tractor in the middle of the night. So many nights, for so long, I could feel Peter standing by my bed and even hear his breathing. Over the years, they had done an excellent job with the ghost stories. Yes, ghosts were real...Peter was still here.

Peter was to be buried the day after. One of the boys came to me with the news that Jack was digging Peter's grave. I was stunned. No! They wouldn't do that. This boy had to be wrong. I had to look for myself. I walked up a gravel track to the top of a small hill and sure enough, there was Jack, his face twisted with pain and hate and tears streaming down his face. Helpless and hurt, my eyes full of tears for him, I walked away in horror and disbelief.

"You had to beat him, but why this way?"

Years later, the same Jack was deported back to Ireland. He had committed a crime and criminals of his calibre were not wanted in our decent community! Did our decent, law-abiding citizens, who were responsible for his deportation, ever ask why he and many others had become like him? What had been done to his young mind? Why did he hate society and authority? In his own way, he was right. He was behaving the way he had been taught. Who then, was wrong? The pupil or the tutor?

The building went on. The Technical School was well on the way after many weeks of hard work, flies and hot weather. In places, the foundation was 6' deep and about 2'6" wide and all dug with picks and shovels by us boys with the help of poor Old Don. He, like us, was slave labour. He was a human jackhammer and mechanical shovel. The very hard nature of the terrain for the foundations, such as stone and hard clay, was beyond our strength. And this is where Don came to the fore. He was very strong, his arms and chest like steel. With a crowbar and a bucket of water, he would spend one or two days punching a hole through the hard ground, lifting the bar and dropping it and, at the same time, turning it. Then he poured a little water in the hole to soften it. He would do this in all weather.

Don had a mental condition and would often pause and commence talking to himself. With hands on hips and a serious look on his face, he would say, "Stop it or I'll give you a hit. I said, 'Stop it'". He would repeat this three or four times. Sometimes, he would let out a scream and then roll his right sleeve up to his elbow, clench his fist and, with brute force, punch himself several times on the chin, crying out, "Stop it! I said, 'Stop it'". He would then kick himself on the back of the ankle, still crying out, "Stop it."

At times he hit himself over the head with a pick or crowbar or he would take his heavy leather belt, wrap it around his hand and flog himself with the buckle. At first, I thought this amusing, but it did not take me long to realize that this unfortunate man was in the same boat as we were.

Keaney would taunt Don when he had his friends up from Perth, showing them the progress of the building. Poor Don may have been having a good day, laughing and smiling to himself. I remember occasions when, in order to amuse his visitors, Keaney would throw a small stone at the back of Don's neck and say to them, "Watch this."

If Don did not react immediately, he would throw another stone. After several times, he would get the reaction he wanted. In the stifling heat, down in a trench, Don would respond in his madcap manner for his audience of smirking, well-dressed Christians – the cream of the Catholic Church.

Sometimes the ground was so hard, it needed blasting. Naturally, Don was called up to punch a hole with a crowbar. Then Keaney would load the hole with gelignite and we would cover it with pieces of old iron, timber and rocks to contain the blast.

One day for a laugh, we put half a bag of cement on top of the whole thing, just to see what would happen. Don, as he often did, remained close to the hole while we took off and hid to watch the result. This time, it was far better than we expected. When she went up, Don was standing there with a silly grin on his face, waiting for the bang which he always enjoyed. Up she went! The half bag of cement took off like a rocket, went up for about ten feet and then came down, landing on Don's head. He stood there, looking like a Christmas tree, the silly grin still on his face, covered in cement from arse'ole to breakfast. We all roared, even Keaney. Yes, we had our fun moments, those we created. We were just boys at heart and got up to the capers all boys of our age did.

We needed these diversions. There were nearly one hundred boys of different temperaments. At times tension would be high and, of course, we would fight with our fists. Keaney had a solution for this, so he thought. He would stop the fight and quietly say, "Tonight in the hall, boys, with the gloves, after church."

At tea time that night, he would announce the big fight with his Irish humour, something like this: "Ole Biddy Ann Norman, my little brown turd from Carlisle, will be fighting Biddy McGee, me old Irish potato, straight after church. Get the gloves and your seconds ready and, remember, the loser gets six of the best on the backside!"

It was my turn to fight a bigger boy. The 'ring' was made up of four forms we sat on. Stripped down to our shorts, gloves on and sitting in our corners with our seconds – our friends doing their bit – Keaney would announce the start and add, "The first to draw blood wins. The loser knows what will happen."

I was far more frightened of the punishment if I lost than I was of my opponent. I had to beat him and knew that he too, would be thinking the same. I was small and fast, my body was hard, harder than my opponent's whose name was Mike. He worked in the kitchen and I on the building site and by this time I was becoming Keaney's top boy. I knew it would be a let down to Keaney that he would find hard to take and, should I lose, he would belt me far harder than he would have beaten Mike for losing.

"Go!" I stood and shaped up. Mike did the same. But he was wide open and charged me. I knew he did not know how to fight. I stepped aside and he kept going, hitting his head on the wall. As he turned round, dazed, I drove one straight at his nose, knowing I would draw blood and win. It was all over in two minutes. I felt sorry for Mike. With a blood nose and crying, he dropped his shorts in front of everybody, bent over and took six strokes of the strap. I felt for him and wished I hadn't won. But it was a hard school, the hardest in Western

Australia with the hardest masters.

This did not happen very often. If we wanted to fight, we would get out of the way and nobody 'snitched' on you. They dared not. The punishment for 'snitching' was far more painful than anything the Brothers could mete out. The boys took care of that!

We had some very hard fights up there. They were cruel. I see now it was dangerous; however, the release of tension and built-up hate – not for one another, but for our situation – was at times volcanic and we would fight until we dropped. When it was over, bloodied and hurting, we would put our arms around each other. Nothing had to be said. We would both know why this had to happen. We had, for a while, become punching bags for the release of our hate. And it would never be mentioned again.

The common denominators, fear and suffering, had bound us together as a close-knit family, strongly united against the common foe, the slave-driver and bullies we feared and hated and who kept us locked in a labour camp, hidden from the view of the outside world, the mask of Christian charity always to the fore and presented as such to the outside world.

I observed this pseudo display on many occasions when Keaney's benefactors would be invited up, seemingly as Christian observers who cared for our welfare and the progress of the Keaney monument. But, in fact, I realized they were there for no other reason than to get into the bush for a game of two-up and a roaring 'piss party'.

In 1949 the polio scare was at its height. Because he feared we may catch the virus and be unable to work on the building, the true reason for his concern, he would, when expecting visitors, have nearly one hundred of us packed on the back of the old 1937 Ford truck, probably still with stones or sand in the bottom and, with a box full of bread and jam sandwiches, tea, sugar and milk and a four gallon kero tin for a billy, we would be carted off to Bunji for a so-called picnic.

We would usually get back by five o'clock and the scene would always be the same. The wooden five gallon keg of beer would be lying empty on the ground and all and sundry would be drunk, singing and carrying on with the usual 'bullshit'.

"What a great man Keaney was. What a great job he was doing. How fortunate we were to be led into a glorious future by such a man."

We had to listen to this endless crap propelling the magnificent Irish giant to the heights. I was old enough to know and think, "You stupid, drunken bastards! You idiots! Your eyes and heads must be full of shit! Do you honestly believe that?"

We would then be assembled in the formation of a choir and made to sing the songs they requested, the conductor probably the drunken clown of the party and who, the next morning, because of his wealth and position, would, in his tailored suit, relate to the staff at his office the sacrifice he had made in visiting the unfortunate orphaned boys at Boys Town.

No doubt these were good people and they meant well but, at the time, I could not see that. I saw only the mockery of what I had been taught and it added further confusion to my already confused mind and increased my contempt for all things supposedly decent. Another zephyr to the rising storm.

Then along came a change – the arrival of six Spanish Nuns from the Abbey at New Norcia, another Catholic institution twenty two miles further north. The Nuns were to free us from our domestic chores so that we could work harder on the building. We knew of New Norcia and had been there to play cricket. It had been founded by a Don Salvado in the 19th Century. It was run by Spanish Priests, Brothers and Nuns and catered for black and white – the whites the paying students, the blacks the less fortunate.

With these Nuns came a further attraction – four good looking, well formed aboriginal girls, about fifteen or sixteen years old. They were beautiful and so were four of the Spanish Nuns who would not have been much older than the black girls. The fronts of their habits and dresses were pushed out beautifully by well moulded breasts. The girls had lovely dark eyes that feasted on the good looking boys around them. But still, with our training, the Nuns were Saints and to be treated as such. So too, the lovely girls. I did not know a thing about sex or women – only that they were built differently to me and stirred something up and these Nuns and girls were certainly doing that!

It was a big day, the day of their arrival, made bigger by

'Trumpet Arse' Joe Norman at the welcoming mass being solemnly said for this very special occasion. Joe, without a doubt, had the most musical anus I had ever heard. The noises would sound like thick custard being forced from the fingers of a rubber glove with bronchitis – a different note being produced by each finger. The newly arrived Nuns were up front with the black girls, the Brothers, as usual, across the back. Mid-way through the Mass, during the raising of the Holy Eucharist, the most solemn part of the ceremony, you could hear a pin drop, the organ playing softly in the background.

It was just a little squeak at first, forced gently out of the small finger of the glove, then two other fingers joined in with a little more force than the first and, with a distinct flowing rumble and on a different scale, then in came the trumpet to complete the loudest, most musical fart I have ever heard. It was magnificent!

I was sitting directly behind Joe. He looked around, caught my eye and gave me a sly, knowing grin. Father Eugene froze, I laughed, a lot of the boys tried to suppress their laughter, the black girls giggled, the Nuns blushed and Keaney cleared his throat so loudly he stifled the last notes of the fart.

I thought Joe and I would get a flogging but it would be worth the laugh we got. But, strangely, not a word was said about it then. However, a month later, Keaney said to Joe and me, "A nice piece of Irish music in Church the other day, boys."

Talking of these Nuns, a boy told me that one day he accidently walked in to a Brother's room and he was chock-a-block up one of the Nuns. In order to keep him quiet, she would let him screw her too. I have no doubts about this. Tony had no reason to lie to me about it and I knew he was telling me the truth. He also told me that another boy was screwing one of the other Nuns. The same Sister herself admitted to me that she was in love with him.

I missed out badly. Another one of the Sisters would grab me by the wrists, at chest height, and try to wrestle with me. Often she would pull my hands into her breasts so that I would graze them. I wondered why her face became flushed every time she did this. Of course, today I know! But it is too late now! I could have had her. She was beautiful with those two little lumps that stuck out on both sides of her habit at chest height. Although I was naive and frightened, I was good looking and had a well formed, athletic body. Yet I did not try anything.

Over the years, my self-esteem had been crushed and I felt ugly. Because of this, I also missed out on making love to two of the aboriginal girls, Violet and Winnis. I loved both of them and they could never take their eyes off me. Violet would leave love notes under my pillow when she made the beds. Some of the boys were having it off with the girls, but I found out too late – eight years too late! I had long left Bindoon.

Naturally, I was going through puberty, but it was never explained to me that this was part of the process of changing from a boy to a man; that mutual masturbation was not unusual; that it was not a mortal sin. I only knew that I had to tell Father about it in the confessional or risk going to Hell forever. I was never told saying a million prayers of Indulgence every day would not alleviate my sexual feelings and the Pope, Mary or all the Saints put together could do nothing about it, even if I prayed for the rest of my life. It was evil and a Mortal sin. The terrible struggles that went on between my hand, my erect penis, my heart and my conscience left me with a great feeling of guilt and self-loathing. Nobody ever told me that sex was a God-given gift and that, used correctly, was natural and beautiful.

We had got over the arrival of the females when two Italian craftsmen, Sinico and Prittorio, landed on the scene on the two-year migration contract applicable in those days. They were craftsmen, both in their own right. Pio excelled in marble, mock marble, mouldings of any description, terrazzo and fine detail work. Prittorio was equally as good in stone work, plastering, concrete and anything at all connected with these skills.

The foundations of the technical school had been laid and the cement brick and stone walls, under the guidance of Joe Pascoli, were almost up to first floor height. As the structure was of Spanish architecture, it was ready for a lot of fine detail work – hence Pio and Pritto.

When they arrived, I was working full time on the building. I was going well at it, laying bricks and stones, plastering, concreting, laying steel, scaffolding and the rest.

Pio set up a workshop in the basement of the new building and when I got a chance I would go down and watch him work. At first, I didn't have a clue what he was doing as I had never seen anything like it before, but I soon found out from his assistant, Tommy Morley, that he was making moulds for the caps and bases of the round columns and cutting the templates to run the big external cement cornices – all shapes and sizes. I would watch Pio, fascinated. He was a genius. Sometimes he would raise his head and catch me watching him, my eyes and mouth wide open. Then he would give me a friendly smile and wink. I liked this man and what he was doing and made up my mind, when I could pluck up the courage, to ask Keaney if I could work in the workshop with Pio. I did not like my chances. I was slowly becoming Keaney's right-hand man, as he put it. So I remained where I was.

The building was a big structure, H shaped. The two legs of the H – the ends – would have been forty feet long by eighteen feet wide and the centre section fifteen feet by thirty. Getting material to first floor height was difficult enough. The bricks were thrown up by what we called a human chain. We positioned ourselves on the scaffold at varying heights, no more than an arm's length away from each other, forming a chain from the ground up. We could then, one at a time, hand the bricks to each other all the way to the top. For the first floor, all the material was got up in this fashion – bricks, stones, mortars and steel – the lot! It was always a hive of activity and very hard work, as none of us had ever done this sort of thing before.

Francis Paul was always there, seated on a chair, very close to the action. I would bet, at the time, that he knew exactly how many of everything went into that job each day. He did not miss a trick. He sat there, winter and summer. Bare headed in summer, he could always be spotted by his shock of white hair and in winter, just as easily by a multi-coloured tea-cosy which he always wore to keep his head warm.

I wondered how he was going to get the material to the next floor. It proved easy for him but not for us. Nothing ever was. We built a huge timber ramp from the ground to the first floor. It was about thirty feet long and seven feet wide. There was no handrail – we had never heard of them – not even on the scaffold!

All the material was sited at the foot of the ramp. A gin wheel hung about six feet above the top platform. A rope, made by us, was fed through the gin wheel. The end of the rope which held the steel hook went down to the bottom of the ramp, the other end going down through the top platform to the ground. It was ingenious and simple, but hard work as none of the wheelbarrows ever went up there half full. His Lordship made sure of that, as he always sat at the top, checking the contents.

If one did come up not quite full, he would pass a remark such as, "Have you come to look at the scenery, sonny? Fill it up next time!"

The building had to go on, no matter the size or age of the boys, no matter the cement and lime burns on the feet for lack of any kind of footwear, the blazing heat, the freezing cold or the cuts and skin-torn hands. He would make us tough in more ways than one with this harsh treatment. And we hated him and all the rest of them, Nuns and all. They were all painted with the same Papal brush.

It was all tough slog and it is difficult to say which was the hardest job. Pouring the concrete slab for the first floor would be one of the hardest and it had to start early in the morning to ensure a continuous pour as a break would weaken the slab. This I understood, for Pio, in his best English, had explained it.

There was no school on these occasions. Every available pair of hands was needed, from the biggest to the smallest. Everything had been made ready the night before for a start straight after breakfast and nobody, just nobody, dared be late. It was six of the best after the day's work if you were. We ran to take up our various positions. For us, it was a challenge and a test of endurance between one another, but we all knew, with pride, that even the smallest would be there at the end of the pour. We older and stronger boys, with the experience, would make sure of that. We would nurse and encourage them and hide them from Keaney. We knew how to do it. He would not get the chance to humiliate one of them, our little brothers as they had become by now. We were a close-knit family and 'They' were the enemy.

My part of this job was to mix the concrete, by hand, all day with the help of three other boys. The four of us stood by the huge pile of blue metal, sand and cement and waited, along with the rest of the boys for the Master to give the order to start. Seated on his chair, this time at the bottom of the ramp to make sure the precious cement was measured out correctly, he would clear his throat and say, "O.K. me old biddies. Show me if you can do it." We hoped our bare feet would last all day against the cement burns.

By hand, the whole operation was carried out in clock-like fashion. Five barrows of metal, two and a half of sand and one wheatbag full of cement were tipped into a heap. The heap was then turned completely over by two of us, then turned back the other way by another two boys. The heap was then pulled out to form a big circle of the dry material and a smaller boy would tip the exact amount of water into the ring. The four of us would then turn it over again twice, as we did the dry and then spade it into a good consistency. It would then, by the same four boys mixing, be shovelled into a wheelbarrow.

Two boys would be behind the barrow and one in the front holding the rope with the hook attached. He would fix the hook to the front of the barrow, the two behind would get between the shafts and start to push, and, at the same time, another boy would yell out, "Pull!"

That was the signal for the two boys at the bottom of the ramp, on the other end of the rope, to pull like hell. They would be doing their very best, knowing the hard job their two mates would be having, pushing the barrow up that long ramp. When it got to the top of the ramp, a waiting lad would immediately whip the hook off the front. Another lad, at the same time, would take over with a stiff, long, steel hook and help with this to where it had to be tipped. There it would be spread out by two or three others and finished off by Pio and Pittorio. We worked like this all day, stopping only for a lunch break. When we finished the section we had to do that day it was close on dark. Very tired and sore, we washed up and went to have our tea. It was bread and milk!

We were very hurt. All day long we had laboured in the hot sun and had extended ourselves to the very limit of endurance and we had hoped that Keaney might get the Sisters to put on something a little special that night, just to show he cared and was proud of us. But it was not to be. We were growing boys, working hard and the meagre plate of bread and milk hardly touched the sides, it was eaten so quickly. Always, we left the table feeling hungry.

How could I get square with this bastard, for all of us? I know. Hadn't we older boys erected all the form work for this slab? We understood its structure or at least, I did. And weren't there two more large sections to pour on the very next day? I'll fix you, you bastard and hurt you where it will hurt the most – your bloody ego and the precious cement you have to beg for. (In those days, cement was worth its weight in gold.) I did not tell a soul what I was about to do. If I were caught, nobody else would get hurt and Keaney would not be able to belt the truth out of anybody else.

After tea, I slipped away to the site. Though it was dark, it mattered little. I knew where every stick of timber was, especially the wedges under the main props. However, I was scared. If I were caught, I would be flogged mercilessly. It was quiet and dark. I had to loosen the wedges as quietly as I could. Easy – a hessian cement bag would dull the noise...I hope the hell it does...anyway, here goes. To beat Keaney, I had to risk it.

I stood directly under the beam of the main slab, right in the centre, bent down and I felt for the wedges, my nerves taut and my knees shaking. With a brick and a bag to dull the noise, slowly and quietly I loosened the main wedges under the props that would bear the most stress. It did not take long in time, but it felt like for ever. Nobody had seen me or heard me, thank God, and I went back to mix with the boys in the games they were playing.

The next morning, the same routine. Keaney seated on his chair, full of pride for the job done the day before. Once again, he gave the order to start. My back bent over the shovel, I looked at him with scorn and hate.

"I will beat you if it kills me, for what you are doing to us."

We slaved away all day and I waited for the crash. It should have gone by now. Perhaps I hadn't eased the wedges enough. The slab was nearly finished. Keaney had won again. He was sitting on his chair, egging us on.

"Just a couple more barrows, boys, then you can knock off."

He had finished speaking when the noise came, the noise that I had waited and prayed for all day.

A mighty crash and thud! Keaney went green. Without him knowing, I observed him and felt like a giant.

"Got ya, you bastard!"

When he realized what had happened, he went berserk and started lashing out with the walking stick he always carried. He caught a couple of boys around the head, but we had seen this performance many times and were soon out of his reach. He cursed and swore in a manner not becoming a Man of God. He was nonplussed and stunned. He blamed everything and everybody, but did not know and never found out that his blue-eyed right-hand man had beaten him. Goliath had been beaten by the moving of a few small wedges!

I felt good. As big and powerful as he was, he could be beaten.

So that the precious concrete was not wasted, we shovelled it onto the back of the Dodge ute and, after many trips and nearly dark, laid a new floor in the piggery. I felt elated. Only I had the knowledge of what had happened. From this I learned a very powerful lesson, one which I shall never forget. Muscle is naught against the power of the brain. To quote Oscar Wilde: "By the displacement of an atom, a world may be shaken."

Another ingenious idea at Bindoon was the hand barrow. It worked on the same principle as the hospital stretcher, only it was made of timber and had many uses. Its main purpose was for carting rocks up the ramp. This task employed five boys. A big rock would be rolled onto it – and I mean big! It would probably take three of us to roll it on. Having done this, four of us would take a handle each and then all lift together. The fifth lad had the most important job – to make sure it did not roll off. And away we would go up the ramp, like something out of the Stone Age and hoping the size would meet the Master's approval on arrival at the top. Should it not, he would let us know with a statement such as, "Where did you get that pigeon egg? Next time, bring a bigger one or you'll take it back."

We did not dare answer back, or even grunt. To have done so would have brought on wrath and of course, the strap.

Although we got the stones for the structure from the paddocks, the cement bricks were not got from there. They were made, by hand, by a boy called Cecil O'Laughan. He was a strapping boy, though not over-burdened with the grey stuff, but he made up for it in physical strength. It was not a rare thing for Cec to make a thousand bricks a day on his own. He took personal pride in this, the only boy ever to have done it. Some of us tried to break his record but we were not in the race. Keaney was aware of this and played on it, always egging him on to a higher tally. Not, I may add, to boost the lad's ego, but simply to speed up production. Cec would always try to better his record, even if it meant starting early or working back.

He did the lot. He mixed his own cement by hand, stacked and cured the bricks and repaired the pallets. And he did the maintenance to his beloved machine that punched out four bricks at a time and assured him forever of his title "King". He loved it and we respected him. The Brothers played on it.

The same boy also held for a long time, the record for the most bags of cement to be taken out of the cement works at Rivervale, a suburb of Perth. Every Friday, Honk would drive the old '37 Ford truck to Perth for the stores and always two boys went with him to go to the cement works. While Cec was at Bindoon, he always went. He was the best. On his return, we would always ask, "How many bags, Cec?" Full of pride, he would tell us.

But Francis Paul was never satisfied, always saying, "See if you can do better next week, sonny."

They got the precious cement for the price of a few eggs, a couple of rabbits which we had dug out, a couple of pounds of butter made by the boys and the cheap slave labour of two fifteen year old boys. It was every boy's dream to go to the cement works for a few reasons, such as a trip to Perth, a day away from Bindoon and, of course, the decent tucker. It was looked on as a picnic – the fact that it was a hard day's work never entered into it. Hard work had become second nature and you were considered to be grown-up if you went to the cement works.

My turn came. I thought it never would as Keaney now

considered me 'top dog' on the building site. Under the guidance of Prittorio, I was supervising the rest of the boys. Perhaps Keaney wisely knew that the break would do me good, for I was to go with my best mate, Joe Norman, who had been there many times before.

Friday morning, at 6.30, we were on the back of the truck, our prized possession being the sugar bag that held our tucker – two tins of bully beef, half a loaf of dry bread, some tea and sugar and a small billy-can. I was happy and Joe was happy for me. We tucked under the tarpaulin on the back of the truck. The world was our oyster and Joe told me the ins and outs of the cement works. The most important was that if we finished early, we could pinch a couple of the men's push-bikes and go for a spin.

Two hours later, we arrived at the Swan Portland Cement works armed with our tucker bag and eighty wheat bags to put the cement in. One wheat bag held two and a half times more than the normal ninety six pound paper bag of cement, which made the average weight of one of these wheat bags, when full, over two hundred pounds and a struggle to manage. Although fairly small, we were strong and intended to break Cecil's record of sixty-five bags. Joe and I were well respected and looked up to by the other boys. If anybody could break the record, they reckoned we could. So we owed it to them as well as ourselves to do just that. Without more ado, we set about it.

The cement we were to collect was from the droppings all over the works, mainly from the conveyer belts which passed through a series of tunnels, from the pits below the chutes and sweepings off the floor. Joe took me to the first pit, a hole about four feet square.

"We take it in turns, Spoug. You go down for one bag, then me. You can't stay down longer than that. You won't be able to breathe."

Down I went and stepped into cement up to my knees. Joe sent the bucket down on the end of a rope. I filled it up and he heaved it to the top, tipped it into the bag and sent it down again. Joe was right. After the first bucketful, it was difficult to breathe. I would be glad to get out. It did not take us long to get about fifteen bags out of there, then to the next pit and the same procedure. We emptied both pits.

Now to the hard part, the tunnels. They were long, narrow and about two feet six inches high. Inside them ran the endless rubber belts that conveyed the cement to various parts of the plant and, of course, there would be the droppings and this is what we were after. We crawled in with a bag and shovel, one holding the bag open, the other, on his knees, getting it in the bag the easiest way possible. When the bag was half full, we dragged it out and topped up another one with it.

We worked like Trojans. We had to break Cecil's record and get a ride on the bikes. After a feast of bully beef and real tea, heads down and arses up, we got into it again. By 2.30 we had seventy five bags all tied up, stacked by the ramp and waiting for Honk to come back at 3.30.

Elated and showered, we ran round to the back to knock off a push bike and hope to hell the owner did not catch us! And to be sure, we picked the flashiest ones with the most gears. Not that we knew what the gears were for, but they sure looked good. And for the next half hour or so, waiting for Honk, we gave those two bikes a real work over.

Honk got back and could not believe we had so much cement. We put on what the old truck would take with everything else that was already loaded on it. He would have to pick up the remainder the next Friday.

All he said was, "How many empty bags have you got?"

Not a word of praise. We had at least expected that. But it did not matter. We were used to that sort of treatment. We would be heroes when we got home. And we were!

Building was always the primary task. But there were others that had to be done and somehow fitted in, and as always, the Master found the solution, regardless of the physical or mental cost to us.

The firebreaks had to be burnt to protect the property, but when? Easy. Instead of recreation time after evening church, the older boys, those working full time, would be loaded on to the back of the old Ford armed with a wet sack each. Also aboard would be a 44 gallon drum filled with water which had a two-fold purpose – first to slake our thirst and second, to keep the bags wet. Sure, there was a water bag strapped to the saddle of the horse the Master always rode on these occasions – a big chestnut draught-horse called Ralph. He looked like something out of the Napoleonic Wars but with a walking stick instead of a gun. And he may well have been Napoleon himself, as he rode up and down the lines of his firebreaker troops until perhaps one or two o'clock in the morning. Then, very, very tired, we would return home to bed, but still rising at the usual time of six o'clock to face the daily chores and abuse.

Then came a real bushfire, one that threatened the property, and all of us, from the biggest to the smallest were to fight it. I had never seen the like of it before and to me the towering clouds of thick black smoke and flames took my mind back to the frightening experience of the manhole to the furnaces when I was six years old. I was scared and wanted to run, but knew I could not, nor dare not. It was an awesome sight.

We were all mustered together. Two of the boys put one of the horses in the dray and the 44 gallon drum went on the back. It was filled with water and a bag put over the top to prevent spillage. Keaney's horse was saddled up and we waited for the rest of the Brothers to join. We stood there silently – one hundred and one of us, each trying to control the fear that was welling up, looking at the billowing smoke, then back to one another. It was then I looked to Keaney and realized, though he be harsh and tough on us, in himself he was strong. He showed no fear and, as always, was confident. I sensed he had done this before and knew what it was about and exactly what to do. He looked the part, seated on the big horse and, despite my fear, I knew I could trust him.

"Come on, me old Biddy Anns, let's go and fight the fire. Listen to the Brothers and do exactly what you are told. You bigger boys take care of the little ones and don't let them out of your sight."

My friend, Joe Norman, looked at me, his expression returning the same message as I conveyed to him – fear, apprehension, determination and pride.

"Let's go, Spoug."

Like a small army, the white-haired General leading on his horse, we set off over the paddock to burn a break back into the oncoming fire. Now that we were moving, it did not seem so bad, the Brothers telling us what to do as we went along and reassuring us that they had done this before and it was common in the Australian bush.

Was this re-assuring talk because they cared for us as people? That they really cared for our physical well-being? That we could be seriously hurt in the fire? Or was it because they wanted only to save the property? This wafted through my mind. I had been deceived many times in the past. I wanted to accept the former but they had not earned my trust. I knew only that I had to rely on them to know what they were doing.

We got closer to the fire. The main front was about half a mile away but not so the heat and the noise, nor the smoke. They were right there with us, and so was the fear. In my mind the lid of the manhole was being lifted off again. Then, I had seen a small part of Hell. Now, it was staring me in the face!

"God, if this is what it's like, I hope I've said my prayers. I hope I told the Priest everything at confession last time."

My mind was full of frightened thoughts but I was soon brought back to reality when Keaney yelled, "Form a long line here, grab a dead bush and light it. Face the oncoming fire and light the ground in front of you. But whatever you do, whatever happens, don't let it get behind you. Beat it out first."

It sounded easy, but a light wind was bringing the fire our way and with it the heat that was making me retch and the smoke that was burning my eyes and throat.

God, this was power! In front of me was a massive wall of flames claiming everything in its way, climbing up the sides of trees with terrible speed. I was amazed and frightened, watching it run up a very tall tree, using the dead bark as its ladder, then the mighty explosion as it hit the foliage, perhaps a hundred feet up and the voluminous clouds of smoke that went with it. Then the wind would carry it along at this height and the flames would reach out to claim another and another tree top. It was coming closer, the heat more intense, almost unbearable. Likewise, the fear that gripped me and, had it not been for my strict training over the years, I would have fled the scene. Keaney was always at hand, astride his horse and yelling, "Pray to Mary and to the Saints for the wind to change. If it doesn't, get ready to run!"

"Fuck Mary, the Saints and you too, Keaney, you mad bastard! Let's get the hell out of here!"

The fire was getting closer, almost on top of us! The wind, though not strong, was bringing the fire near enough to jump the break and, if it did, we would have to run for our lives.

I prayed like hell and I am sure all the other boys did too. We toiled like Trojans to beat out the flames of the break we had already lit so that they did not get behind us, lest we be trapped – and also to protect our bare feet. We were spread out, probably along a half mile front, Keaney riding up and down giving orders, not only to the boys, but also to the Brothers. We were hot, tired and black.

We prayed: "Please change the wind. We can't go on much longer."

My arms were aching, my feet were hot and aching too and the heat was making me vomit.

Somebody must have heard us, for I felt the wind on my back. It had turned and was blowing the break back to the main fire. Thank God, it was over and nobody had been hurt. We had felt the power, heat and fury, not only of nature but also of Hell, and were reminded of this many times after when we misbehaved.

Another very hard and back-breaking task was stooking the sheaves of hay. All day in the blazing sun, the stubble cutting our bare feet, we worked at stooking, loading them onto the truck and then into the haystack. We worked all day in the blazing sun. I hated this work and longed to go back to the building site. As hard as that was, I had become accustomed to it and liked it. It was creative. This farming was for the peasants.

At the same time the main building project went on, held together by the Italians and a skeleton crew. It was well on the way, the second floor walls nearly scaffold high and looking like a technical school.

But relentless Keaney never gave up. There was always another project and always as hard as the last one. This time it was a new concrete water tank on the hill. We levelled the site with horses and scoops, poured the slab floor – all by hand – formed the walls, tied the steel and poured the concrete in the same manner as we did the main building slab, the difference being we could not tip the concrete into the framework. We had the backbreaking job of putting it in by bucket. We did this from early morning until one lift of the formwork was full. It mattered not what time we finished or how tired or hungry we were. There could not be a break in the wall of the tank at any cost as it would leak. For six solid days we worked relentlessly, Saturday and Sunday included, until the tank, thirty feet in diameter and eight feet high, was completed. We were proud of ourselves, but never got thanks or a word of praise for a job well done, only constant abuse and the threat of a hiding should one look like slacking.

One must hand it to those people. They were well trained in driving people to the very limit of endurance and, at the same time, humiliating them, and inducing in their victims a feeling that they should be grateful for what was being done for them. They fed and clothed us and kept a roof over our heads, but above all, they were bringing us up in the best Catholic tradition and thus forming our minds, hearts and morals to enter the world as upright citizens and fine examples of Christianity and Catholicism.

Francis Paul excelled here. "How would you like a new sports ground, boys? All your own."

Great! He allocated a piece of flat, virgin bush, heavily timbered with red and white gum and dense undergrowth and known as the Tablelands.

"That's yours and it will be your project. You can clear it and burn it in your spare time after school and on the weekends, but it must not interfere with the building project."

It sounded like a great idea. Our own sports ground, made by us! And we went for it – all of us. From nine to sixteen years old, all working together, talking about the Test matches and soccer finals between England and Australia that we would organise when the ground was finished. We worked bloody hard at it.

One Brother, a brilliant mechanic, the one who had slipped his hand up my shorts a few times, got the ex-army tank going. With this, he bashed down all the big trees. When he had finished, we went to see it. Shit! It was a big sports ground, around fifteen acres. Gee, they were good to us! They've given us all this ground for a sports field. All we have to do is clear and burn it.

Every weekend for months, we went up there and worked our hearts out. We would take three or four of the old draught horses. By this time, we were familiar with them and knew how to harness, handle and work them. We knew their individual capabilities, their characters and strengths. We never hurt them. They were strong and gentle. We loved them and told them, "This is our new sports ground. You've got to work extra hard for us."

They seemed to know and gave us their best. We would snig them to a huge log with the snigging chains and say, "Come on! This is a big one. Pull it for us."

The beautiful animal would feel and sense the weight of the load. If it was extra heavy, it would dig its hooves into the ground, bend its hind legs, dig the front hooves in then lean forward and take a bite. Should the log not move, it would bend its rump nearly to the ground and, encouraged by our words and pats on the head, give a grunt and move the log to the pile we were making and getting ready to burn. We always gave the horses a cheer after such an achievement. They knew it and loved it. We had a tremendous empathy with them.

We piled all the fallen trees this way. Then we would heap all the smaller sticks on a big timber sled we had made and, drawn by horse, take it to the pile and use it for starting wood to set fire to the pile. This was our ground. We were fussy, going over it carefully and leaving it as clean as a swept floor. It looked good and the wicket, the goal posts and thousands of people who would come to see us play a test match against New Norcia were getting closer. The sacrifice of many weekends, sore hands and feet, sweat and tears would soon all be worth it. In went the plough and harrows; the clover and grass were planted and we waited for permission to use our new field.

It never came. The sheep and cattle were turned in on it and until I left, that ground saw only the feet and arseholes of cattle and what fell out of them. Never was it graced with a cricket ball, stumps, goal posts nor any of the huge crowds of our youthful imaginations. It had been just another con, and a very clever one at that! Another big coal to add to the fire of hatred and contempt. A bitter blow, not left unrecorded by the computer inside my head. The garbage bin was getting close to overflowing.

But there was Christmas time and the Christmas holidays to look forward to. All the boys, save six, were piled on to the back of the Ford with big ex-army tents, the gear they needed and shunted off to a place called Moore River, where they would spend two weeks.

I was one of the six, my job to cook for the people left behind – five Brothers, four staff and five other boys. I knew the ropes as this was my second stint at it. I was approaching my fifteenth birthday. I would rise at half past five, awakened by the clock which I was always frightened would not wake me. If it failed, I would get a flogging. I would light the two old wood stoves in the kitchen and then begin preparing two separate breakfasts. The Brothers and staff always ate differently to the boys. Porridge for the boys; for the others, special porridge followed by bacon or chops and eggs or whatever. This I served at seven o'clock to all of them. After breakfast I would wash up and get ready for morning tea at ten o'clock as well as prepare for lunch, which was at twelve o'clock. I also set both tables in the two separate dining rooms. The Brothers and staff always ate apart as did the Nuns, although they were not there at Christmas time. After lunch, there was another wash-up, the pots in the kitchen to clean followed by preparation for the evening meals. Two separate meals made a difficult task twice as difficult. Tea at six o'clock, wash up, set the tables for breakfast the following morning, clean out the stoves and set the fires and then make sure the kitchen was left spotless. After that, I had to prepare supper for nine o'clock for the Brothers only and then probably cut down a sheep for the next day's meat. I did this, seven days a week for two weeks. I was strong and used to hard work, but those long hours nearly killed me. At nine or ten o'clock, I would crawl into bed and pray the alarm would wake me.

Once, I did not set it for what I thought was a very good reason, but not so Keaney!

It had been a hard day in the kitchen. I was tired and nearly finished when in walked 'Pinky' Hayes from Perth. He was a friend of Keaney and we liked him, one of the few we did like. Pinky often came up to shoot rabbits and every time he came he would bring something for the boys, either comics or chewing gum. He was a nice man although his girl was even nicer. I cannot remember her name, so will call her June.

They came into the kitchen. "How about coming shooting, Spoug?"

"I'll get into trouble, Pinky. I haven't finished my work."

"She'll be right," said Pinky. "I'll tell Brother Keaney. He told me to ask you and 'Chicken' O'Connor to come, anyway. So come on."

I was delighted – a ride in his big Chevvy car, a break from the kitchen and a chance to drool over his lovely lady. To hell with Keaney and everything else. Right, let's go.

'Chicken' was already in the back of the big black '48 Chevvy, chewing on the gum Pinky had given him, lying back in the seat and doing his best to look like a snob in his dirty khaki shorts and shirt. I hopped in beside him, accepted a chewy and we took off.

June held the spotlight, Pinky drove and we all looked for rabbits. That wasn't hard as, in those days they were in plague numbers. We had not gone far when the car was stopped and Pinky took a shot, making a kill. I flew out of the car and ran like hell to pick up the kill in the near darkness, the only light coming from the spotlight. My shin ran into something and there was a sharp crack. The pain ran right through my body. I thought Pinky had shot me in the leg! I went down in agony. The three of them raced to me and bent over as I was lying on the ground. Although I tried not to cry, the hot tears of pain were running down my cheeks. They picked me up and carried me back to the car as gently as the ground permitted and drove me back to Bindoon.

It was late when we got back and everybody was in bed, including Keaney. June was a nurse. She made me as comfortable as possible and said, "You'll be alright. They'll take care of you in the morning." She gave me a kiss and left. I was so tired that I slept, in spite of the agonising pain.

I was awakened by Chicken with these words: "You'd better get up to the kitchen, Spoug. Keaney's goin' mad because there's no breakfast and he's flogging shit out of Cassidy because he can't cook."

"Tell him there's something wrong with my leg. It hurts and I don't think I can walk on it."

Chicken was scared. He did not want to take the news back to the already berserk Irishman. No doubt he would get a serve of the walking stick too. But he left and it was not long before he returned with another boy, Charlie Penglaze. They were both very frightened.

"He said we have to carry you up, Spoug and you can sit down and tell Cassidy what to do."

As gently as they could, my two friends carried me to the kitchen and gave words of encouragement and comfort. Tears came to their eyes as they saw my face screwed up in pain.

"You'll be alright, Spoug. He won't hit you – not with a broken leg."

There was no fear in me. I was sure he wouldn't either. We got to the kitchen, some five hundred yards away, but long before we got there, I could hear the lunatic going off his head and poor Cassidy screaming. What my thoughts were then, I cannot recall. Probably a mixture of hate and contempt. The boys took me into the kitchen and sat me on the edge of a table. By this time, my lower leg and foot were swollen and my foot was taking on a bluish colour. Keaney stood in front of me, his face contorted in rage and I knew he was capable of anything in this frame of mind. I had seen it often before. But strangely, I had no fear, as bad as he could be. Surely he would not hurt me in this state of helplessness.

"What's wrong with your leg?"

"I think it's broken, Brother."

"Can you move your toes?"

"Yes."

"Then it's not broken. You left last night to go rabbit shooting without finishing your work, and this is God's punishment for that."

He spoke through gritted teeth, his voice full of vehemence and I sat there, helpless, crying from the agony in my legs as this giant of a man – to the outside world the personification of everything Christian and decent – towered over me and threw abuse at me.

"You little black shit, you brown turd, you walking bag of

shit. May God damn you to hell-fire and you burn there forever."

He had worked himself into a frenzy with these words. He raised his great arm and, with a force that sent me backwards on the table, he backhanded me across the mouth. I cannot describe my feelings in depth – that would be impossible. The hurt in my leg and the blow to my face was nothing in comparison with the hurt and disbelief I experienced at that moment. But it gave me a strength and courage I had never known before. I sat up and for the first time in my life, looked one of these bastards in the eye and exposed the pain and hate of nearly thirteen years of suffering.

He read what they said. "One day you will pay for this. I will run away and you will never find me. You will never bring me back here. I will kill myself before you do. You will never get the satisfaction of humiliating me like this ever again. I swear to God you won't. I am a human being and helpless against you. This time Keaney, you have gone too far. You will never do this to me again."

It was with the courage that hate brings, that I looked him straight in the eye and simply said, "ONE DAY I WILL BEAT YOU!"

He knew exactly what I meant. His reply told me that.

"Don't try it, sonny!"

That sentence made up my mind. He had thrown me a challenge and, with perverted glee, I silently took it up.

He then had the boys sit me on the concrete floor in the kitchen, with my back to the wall, to give instructions to the still crying Johnny Cassidy, on how to prepare the meals. All day I sat there and advised him, making sure he never made a mistake and so bring Keaney's walking stick or strap on either of us. The pain in my leg was becoming worse as was the swelling. It was getting bluer. So were my foot and toes. I had been sitting there like that from half past six in the morning and it was now five thirty in the afternoon when the Master stood before me with a brilliant deduction.

"It might be broken, sonny. I'll get one of the staff to run you down to Perth and have it X-rayed."

Somehow or other, with the help of the boys, I got showered and dressed, and was put in the car and driven sixty five agonising miles to the Royal Perth Hospital. On arrival, I was X-rayed. Both shin bones were broken right through. The doctor who was attending me told me he would have to straighten and set the leg and I looked up from the bed and said, "O.K."

Without a painkiller of any sort, he raised my leg up by taking hold of it behind the heel and knee and bringing my foot to eye level. He then looked along the leg as though looking down a gun barrel. "It's slightly bent. I will have to straighten it."

Present were two male orderlies and a lovely little nurse. The doctor nodded to them. The orderlies took a shoulder each, the nurse my other leg and I was pinned to the bed.

The doctor said, "This will hurt."

He wasn't wrong! He then pulled in opposite directions on my heel and knee to part the bones, and still sighting down my leg, slowly twisted until he thought it straight. Oh, the pain! Oh Jesus! I wanted to scream but dare not. He might belt me. As he twisted, I gritted my teeth, the tears running down my face and I was retching it was so painful.

"Hurt much?"

I shook my head. I dare not complain.

"It's not quite straight. I'll have to do it again."

And he did, the cruel bastard. Were all people in authority like this?

As he was setting my leg in plaster, I dared to look up at the lovely young nurse. She had tears in her eyes. "What's she crying for?" She was stroking my head, gently. She must have lost a member of the family or something, to be crying like that or maybe the doctor was going to belt her because she had not done her job properly. The leg had been set and she wheeled me to a ward, put me in a bed, tucked me in and brought me a cup of tea.

"There you are, darling. I know it hurt. You're a brave boy. Normally, they give an anaesthetic when they do that sort of thing. I don't know why they didn't give you one." She stroked me gently on the face, still with tears in her eye. It was totally alien to me. A beautiful young woman really cared about me. But why?

At nine o'clock the next morning, they came and took me

straight back to Bindoon, my leg in plaster from the toes to half-way up my thigh and armed with a pair of crutches. And believe it or not, straight back to the kitchen! With the help of Cassidy, I went about my chores as though nothing had happened, still the same routine as before. Four days later, the boys got back from Moore River and, without further ado, straight back to the construction site, plaster and all!

What was my job? To sit on a stack of bricks on a scaffold, two floors up and supervise the boys. I was fifteen and had become the leading hand as the previous boy had reached sixteen and had gone into the outside world. But Keaney was not happy with this – I was not producing. His best man on the tools was sitting on his arse. That is when he put me in the workshop with Pio, the man whose ability I really admired.

By this time, we could make ourselves understood. The Italians had learned some English and I quite a bit of Italian. I remained with Pio for six weeks while my leg was in plaster and then for another six weeks while the strength returned to my frail leg. I learned many things from him. How to run moulds, cut templates, make terrazzo, build round columns and many other skills. It seemed to be second nature to me. Pio recognised this and gave me plenty of encouragement.

One day, he told me, "Spoug, I had some good boys in Italy, very good boys, but never one as good as you. Stay here at Bindoon. I can make a craftsman out of you."

But I had different ideas. I respected Pio and loved the work and dearly wished to be as good as he was, but not here – anywhere else but here. I was becoming mentally stronger. The past thirteen years had filled me with hate, defiance and contempt and my leg was a good reminder of the promise I had made to myself.

Pio told me, on a number of occasions, that Keaney intended to keep me there and put me on the paid staff after I had turned sixteen. My ideas differed and I strongly suspected that Keaney sensed this. He thought a lot of me and respected my skills and intelligence. I was his leading hand and a valuable asset, one that would be hard to replace on the construction of his monument. I knew it. It was the ace card and I held it. And he knew I did. I also knew that he knew I intended to run away one day. He was smart enough to know the damage he had done to my mind with the treatment of my broken leg. He knew that I looked upon him with contempt for the unjust punishment he had meted out and that I intended, one way or another, to get square for it. He showed me his hand in his change of attitude towards me. He, for once, tried to treat me as a human being but it was too late.

Pio encouraged me to stay on. He could see my potential, but I never shared my intentions with him or anyone else. Not even when he told me that the Brothers were cruel to us; that he did not like what he saw. As soon as his two-year contract was finished, he and Prittorio would be off to Perth to earn the kind of money men of their ability could demand, instead of the pittance that was being paid to them. They were being used and they knew it. It would be a sad loss to the boys and a bitter blow to Keaney when these good, hard working men left. They were kind and considerate and protected us from the wrath of the Brothers if and when they could.

I saw the goodness in them, when, of their own accord and in their own time, they crafted a headstone for the grave of Peter Woods. I watched, in reverence as Pio shaped the piece of marble and, with loving care and skill, cut the name and lettering for our friend's head-stone, using his chisels as easily as though they were pencils. And likewise, Prittorio cut a huge piece of ironstone rock to the shape required, to hold the inscribed piece of marble. It was a lovely piece of work. We wanted to help.

They let us dig the hole and place the concrete at the grave head, in readiness for the beautiful monument they then erected. We loved them for it. Why couldn't the Brothers have done this? They had thrown him in a hole in the ground and remembered him only when they wanted to remind us that his ghost was still around. It was a sad state of affairs. Why weren't the Brothers like these two men?

Why, if we were all one family in the eyes of God, did we eat different food in separate dining rooms? How could Keaney sit in the dining room with us, at his own little table with a lovely tray, silver teapot, toast and marmalade while we ate a plate of watery porridge and drank a cup of tea which had been stewing on the stove all night and which had been fortified with the dregs from the Brothers' teapots the night before. It was rank, to say the least, but it was all we had to drink.

This man, on one occasion, walked around the dining room, stick in hand and threatening a belting to any boy who would not eat the chook mash that had been mistaken for the porridge and then wash it down with the monthly dose of Epsom salts. And on the same morning, pick a small boy up by the scruff of the neck and drop-kick him through the dining room door, cursing as he did so simply because he had broken a plate by tripping on the floor.

How could a grown man pick up a stick and lay it across a small boy's arm with sufficient force to break it, just because he had been innocently singing an Irish rebel song? This man was not the Master but another Brother, the same man who had taken me to his room one night and unmercifully flogged me for not washing my trowel.

Brother O had his own instrument of torture, befitting him as he was a mechanic. It was the fan belt of a truck. The 'offender' would extend his arms and three lashes would be laid upon each, from the fingers to the inside of the elbow, providing, of course, that the victim did not flinch.

They had another cruel and humiliating stunt for the bed wetters. Draping the wet sheets over the offenders' heads so they were completely covered, they were made to stand on the open verandah, like silent ghosts or statues, for all to see. They would be crying, and draped with the wet veil, they would be left standing there, sometimes for as long as three hours.

No, it was not just Keaney who was cruel. They were all good at it! I only mention him the most because I had the most to do with him. He looked after the building site. The other Brothers had their own areas like the carpenter's shop, the mechanic's workshop, the orchard, the farm etc.

Then there was Brother S who looked after the stock. He was a real stockman – long, slim, his skin wrinkled and tanned, a superb horseman and sheepman with his lovely dog, Whisky. Somehow, he was slightly different from the rest. A loner who did not have much to do with us and never used the strap to punish us, he had another method which we soon woke up to.

While dressing you down, calmly and quietly, he would suddenly bring a haymaker up that sent you sprawling. Only one was needed. His arms were long and strong and the hands were like plates of meat and as tough as leather. But we learned to back pedal when confronted by him. Strangely enough, if he failed to connect with the haymaker, he let you go. You had beaten him fairly.

At lambing time he would set baits for the foxes and we were not allowed in the lambing paddocks. No way!

Another good friend of mine, Bob Hare, and I were returning from our rabbit traps and decided we would take a risk by following a short cut through the lambing paddock. We were halfway across when, seemingly out of a hole in the ground, emerged Brother S astride his horse. He was laying fox baits. He would throw a poisoned bit of meat on the ground, then run over it with a piece of smelly sheep gut attached to a length of wire. We ran straight into him. He got off his horse and started to dress us down. We kept our eyes on his hands and slowly back pedalled. Then, out of nowhere – swoosh! The filthy piece of sheep gut hit me right in the side of the face. I had been watching his free left hand, but the cunning old bastard had caught me with his right – the one that held the wire and sheep gut. And why not? He was an ex pug. We bolted but he told Keaney and, of course, we got it.

Brother N was another kettle of fish. He taught boxing and was a fanatic on sports and planting trees all over the place. He would punish with the strap and his fists and always there would be one or two holes to dig through the hard clay, as added punishment. This task had to be done in one's free time. On a couple of occasions that I had to do it, I had to feel my way around in the dark.

He was teaching a boy, Tony Hardigan, to box and came the day that Tony, who had plenty of guts, was easily able to beat him. He was given the treatment from N and told to dig a hole. He dug the hole as ordered and, as always, used water to help soften the clay while digging, which left a sloppy mess in the bottom of the hole. N came to inspect the work. As quick as a flash, Tony drove a left to his gut and followed through with a right to the jaw. Down went N with a grunt. Tony grabbed him by the hair, shoved his head down the hole and rubbed his face in the wet mud at the bottom.

"That's the last hole I'll dig for you, you old bastard."

He walked away and left him there. Henceforth, no further boxing lessons for anyone.

We were getting older and wiser. The wheel was turning. Was God real? Or had they invented him? Was he a Catholic invention that gave people licence to behave inhumanely to their fellow men? Would he be pleased to see half a dozen fifteen and sixteen year old boys loaded on to the back of a semi-trailer, riding behind the cab in the blazing hot sun, stacking it with railway lines, some twenty to twenty five feet long – and in loading, the danger of one slip, perhaps killing or severely maiming one of us? I wonder.....

These railway lines were used as reinforcement in the concrete lintels and the man-handling of them always frightened me. Once again the method of getting them in position was simple but not without danger. This is how it was done. We would pair off, one of the pair grabbing a short length of timber and slipping it under the steel. We would be spaced along each side of it, at about two foot intervals, each pair with a stick between them. When the word was given, we all strained under the heavy load, encouraging each other, well aware of the consequences should one boy's arms or legs give way under the excessive weight – twenty or thirty of us over the side of the ramp, tangled up with a railway line.

It was a frightening thought but we knew each other well and our individual capabilities. Teamwork was of absolute importance. Slowly feeling the weight, we would march up the ramp like something out of the Pharaohs, put it down and, with the help of Don, Pio and Prittorio, man-handle it on to the scaffold, then from there to its place in the beam. Once there, we would all give a sigh of relief.

We had some fun on occasions, like giving each other rides down the ramp on the wheelbarrow, though at times, not without incident. Once, while flying flat out down the ramp with a barrow with a passenger on board, John O'Mara, when about halfway down, lost balance and, at full tilt, he, the passenger and the vehicle went arse over head over the side, about an eight foot drop. Thank God Keaney wasn't there, though when he heard of it, his only comment was, "Is the wheelbarrow alright, sonny?" Not a single query as to the condition of the boys!

The equipment always took priority, especially the barrows. He seemed to have a soft spot for them. Sometimes we would break the shafts and he would go berserk. And at times, at the risk of a flogging, we would purposely break them – another small victory, as it would slow down the project, while the lads in the carpenter's shop made new ones and this hurt Keaney more than the broken shafts.

Then there was the pig bin – another ingenious contraption. It was a 44 gallon drum mounted on a home-made trolley. It was parked outside the kitchen to collect all the food slops. When it was full, it was wrestled down the half-mile slope by one of us. We took it in turns and it was always a challenge to see who could get this drum of slops down the hill in the shortest time. It was very heavy and would take three of us to tip it back to the point of balance, carefully steer it to the top of the hill, making sure the challenger had the best possible chance of steering his drum of muck down the half-mile incline, negotiating a nearly 45 degree bend half-way down and arriving at the piggery with the contents intact. Quite a feat when the whole contraption weighed about four times more than the pilot! But it was fun and we loved it because there was always a good chance the chariot of shit, because of its weight, would gather more momentum than the driver's legs could keep pace with. The thing would start to see-saw and the lad, with a look of determination, would have his legs in mid-air, not missing a stride and knowing if he should get too airborne he would lose control and go straight over the top, to be buried under the drum of shit. He would also risk a flogging for wasting precious food. We would all look on, placing bets to see if he would make it at a speed that was easily 60 miles an hour by the dead reckoning of his barrackers and only 20 by the enemy.

Came the moment of truth. Could he manipulate this crude vehicle round that bend at that speed? And miss the fence as well? We'd be full of excitement and waiting, not to see how fast he made it to the piggery, but for the comical sight of him flying over the handlebars and landing in the drum of muck.

There were many occasions when we were not disappointed.

I had better get back to the building site. The Master is screaming out. He wants forty bags of hot lime slaked off and knocked into a compo. I was responsible for the supervision of jobs such as slaking lime. In those days, lime came in rock form, in hessian sacks and looked just like lumps of limestone. We would measure out four barrows of sand into a heap and then, with shovels and 'larries' we would form a large ring with the sand, tip a bag of lime into the centre and put the hose on it. When wet, it would swell and generate tremendous heat, then start to boil, I suppose like a small volcano.

There were two things we had to remember – not to get it in our eyes and to keep our bare feet out of it. It could burn like hell. When the lime had stopped boiling and had broken up, we would mix it with the sand, then barrow it into a stockpile to blow and mature. It was not unusual for us to slake off fifty or sixty bags in one go, in the same day, not bad for a bunch of small boys when you consider this represents two to five hundred wheelbarrows of mortar. And sometimes we would achieve this in six hours!

I must add here that we did get a bonus when we left school to work full time – a pair of work boots. They were not new. They were ex-army and were kept in a room, in a big pile on the floor, not in pairs and all shapes and sizes. The trick was to select something as close to a pair as possible. One would find two the same size, though one might be black and the other tan. But that did not matter. It was a status symbol. One was now grown up and had left school, so what matter the colour or size?

Time had slipped by and, not without a lot of blood, sweat and tears, the technical school was completed. We were proud of it and why shouldn't we be? Green and inexperienced, frail and many times frightened, pushed often to the limit of endurance, with the help of two caring and skilled craftsmen, Pio and Prittorio, we had raised this lovely building from the hard clay soil to the freedom of the sky.

Opening day, with all pomp and ceremony, was attended by Priests, Nuns, Bishops, the Lord Abbot from New Norcia and the well-dressed 'pillars of the church' from Perth. Every man and his dog were there – Keaney, looked every bit the image they had painted him. He was scrubbed up, his shock of white hair shining. He wore a khaki outfit with highly polished boots and leather gaiters to knee high. He played the part well, cutting a fine and powerful figure.

What these visitors did not know was what that structure had cost us; that the man they were admiring and praising to the heights for his achievement was far removed from the man we knew; that the man who had got this structure erected, had done so with little or no regard for human feeling.

I had foregone the picture show the night before to run his hot bath, wash his hair and back and had spent a long time after the day's work, when the other lads were playing, polishing those boots and gaiters he wore – and not without abuse.

The tables in our dining room were adorned with white table cloths and flowers and shining cutlery; the floors were spotless, prepared especially for the occasion and not without many lost hours of our spare time. The visitors ate in there. We ate outside in the courtyard after fighting over the scraps they had left.

It was a brilliantly presented facade. I stood back and observed the whole performance with contempt. With all the pomp and ceremony, the speeches of praise for Keaney, the Brothers and Nuns, there was not a word of commendation for the boys from any person.

My sixteenth birthday was near. The garbage bin was full and I had not forgotten my promise to myself. By this time it was common knowledge that I would be retained and placed on the paid staff. Pio and Prittorio had taught me well. I was a 'natural' for the building trade and I knew, without conceit, that I was good and would be a sad loss. Francis Paul's attitude towards me was slowly changing; he was beginning to speak to me as an adult and I knew why and relished it.

Two days after my sixteenth birthday, a new Brother arrived, fresh from College, and started to throw his weight around. He did not know what he had walked into. Years of training had made us hard; we could take a flogging without a murmur. We knew the ropes and could stand up to all the Brothers, except Keaney. And in walked this goose. So we tried him out. We laughed in his face, even when he belted us with his strap and strangely enough, Keaney always turned a blind eye.

I felt that he must have warned this turkey, "Watch yourself! You're not dealing with a bunch of ordinary schoolboys here. Learn the hard way and learn it quick or they will break you."

He was a smart-arse and one day he made the mistake I was waiting for. He confronted me over something to do with my job on the site – something he knew nothing about. He knew he lacked the knowledge and had made a fool of himself in front of the boys. Then, to cover up, he tried to make a fool of me.

Full of hate and contempt for this creep, I quietly told him, "Fuck off, you idiot."

He smashed me across the face with a backhander. Hurt, rage and fear came upon me and I remembered my promise to myself: nobody will ever do this to me again and, with all my strength, I hit him in the face and ran to the cheers of the boys. My mind was made up in that instant and nothing could change it.

I mentally turned the key in the lock and threw it away. That night I would run away. It was then about 3 p.m. and I told not a soul of my intentions, for a very good reason.

At 8.30 p.m., I went to bed as usual. From where I slept on the open verandah, I could see straight into Keaney's room and he always left his door ajar. I had observed his movements for nearly twelve months. Night after night, though tired, I would stay awake. The generator supplying the electric power to the place was automatically switched off every night at nine o'clock. Keaney would then light a candle and then read for perhaps another hour. On some occasions he would get up, with candle in hand, and walk the length of the verandah where all the older boys slept – for one reason only – to make sure nobody had shot through as this was his greatest fear. The fear was not for the safety of the runaway but that his pride and public image would be damaged.

Should the absconder not be apprehended, it would be a bitter, disastrous blow. I had known this for a long time. After checking on the boys, he would go back to bed and remain there for the rest of the night.

At first, I fought the urge to sleep and had to remind myself of the importance of the risky action I was about to undertake. Remaining awake was no longer a problem. I waited for what seemed a good hour after he had gone back to bed. It was deadly silent, apart from the breathing of my mates, and quite dark. There was no fear, only quiet determination to beat the bastard. I knew I could. I had done the ground work well. I owed it not only to myself but to all the other boys not to get caught at any price. If anyone could do it, it would be Spoug, they reckoned.

I crept down to my locker, got out a sugar bag and put in it all my worldly belongings – my spare pair of khaki shorts and shirt, a pack of cigs I had pinched from Honk's room, two pears and three apples I had stolen and in my pocket was 1 1/2d. I was dressed in my other khaki outfit, a pair of ex-army boots, no socks and an old slouch hat. For a moment, I stood in the semi-dark locker room and in my mind saw all of us getting dressed for work, winter and summer; saw the madman Keaney coming through the door, waving his walking stick and hitting anybody who was in his way, cursing as he went and we scurrying out at times half-dressed to get away from him and I saw a grim picture of the next morning.

"Spoug's gone!"

All hell would break loose. I knew the boys who would be flogged and I started to cry. My best mates! I felt as though I had betrayed them by not telling them, but my silence was my ace card.

In the semi-darkness, crying and sad for them, I started the lonely one and a half mile walk down the same gravel road I had come up just four and a half years before, at that time excited and full of hope for something better than I had left behind in England. Now I was walking into a world I knew nothing about, unsure as to where I was going or even if I would get there and I felt all alone. They had educated me well in hate and contempt for all things decent. My dreams of a high education in the academics had been smashed and had been replaced by one that twisted my young mind. And they had done it well!

I walked along, many thoughts running through my head, two being prominent – not to get caught and what would happen to my friends in the morning, especially those who had been closest to me. I knew the routine well. As soon as a runaway was discovered, his best friends were given the third degree, intimidated with the stick and forced to tell where he had gone. The Brothers knew these things were always shared with best friends and they always sweated on it and extracted the answer. I had known for twelve months I was going to go and on the occasions when running away was discussed I had strongly hinted which way I would go if and when I did. But I always added that I would probably be too scared to try it, anyway. This last remark was for Keaney's benefit, knowing it would get back to him; indeed, I made sure of it by dropping it in the right places. This would keep him guessing as I had no intention of going the way I had told my friends. Nobody would know when I was going or where I was heading and this was the ace card with which I hoped to beat that bastard.

It was a still, clear night and I walked with a steady, determined step, although in no great hurry. Many thoughts went through my mind. There were no prayers. I had thrown God and the Saints and all the rest of then out the window a long time before. He had to be a cruel, unjust God. If there was another side to Him, I never saw it. Yes, they must have invented Him for their own benefit, to keep control of us by the image of a vengeful God.

And now, here I was, sixteen years old and walking down a lonely road in the middle of the night. All I knew about myself was that I was born in England in 1936, and thanks to Keaney's register, the names of my parents and my place of birth. That was all I knew. But I was free now, and felt it and was determined to remain that way.

I hit the main bitumen road, sat down and waited for a ride in the opposite direction to that which I had told my friends I would go. Would I get a ride? What would I say when I did? If I did not get a ride before daybreak, I would have to go back and try again the next night. How long would I have to wait?

CHAPTER

3

The Worldly Hope men set their Hearts upon
Turns Ashes — or it prospers; and anon,
Like Snow upon the Desert's dusty Face
Lighting a little Hour or two — is gone.
Omar Khayyam

I sat by the road and lit a cigarette, my feelings now calm and determined. The game of chess had begun, the moves carefully calculated over a long period. Only time would tell if my summing up of Keaney had been right. I was David pitting my wits against Goliath. Should my reckoning be wrong, I would be taken back and thrashed. This did not frighten me. They could take me back, but they would never hold me again, not at any cost. It had taken fourteen years of cruelty to get me sitting where I was with these thoughts in my mind. There would be no turning back - even at daylight.

I had been there about ten minutes when an old T-model Ford pulled up.

"Where are you going?"

"To Moora." (About 120 miles up the track.)

"Where are you from?"

I started to spin them a fabricated yarn, but I knew it wasn't going over too well.

They were a young couple with a little baby. Their names were Tom and Laurel and they were on their way to a place called Morawa, nearly 300 miles away. They had friends there and were going to share-farm with them.

So I told them the truth - that I was running away and

why. They suggested I go back, but I told them, quite firmly, "No! If you don't take me, I will wait for somebody who will. I am not going back! NEVER!"

"O.K." Tom said, "Get in."

It was not long before I was asleep.

"Lionel, we're at Moora. Do you want to get out?"

It was Laurel waking me. It was still dark and cold and I was half asleep.

"I don't think you should get out here. Come up to Morawa with us. We may be able to get you a job on a farm with one of our friends."

I agreed and went back to sleep. Waking at daylight, the old T-model Ford was still chugging away. Where was I? Had these people turned round while I was asleep to take me back to Bindoon? I dare not trust anyone. I looked out of the window at strange country I had never seen before. They could not have turned back ... I know, they'll probably hand me over to the cops as soon as we get there. At the first opportunity, I'll bolt.

Tom looked around at me. "How are you feeling? We're going to stop and boil the billy in a minute. Would you like a cuppa?"

I was stunned. They were both smiling at me as though they really meant it and were now offering me a cup of their tea. What was wrong with these people? They were strange and I was frightened and suspicious of them. Maybe they were just setting me up.

They were city people and were amazed when I offered to light the fire and boil the billy for them, which I did in about ten minutes. We sat down on a log. Then another strange thing – Laurel got the food out and told me to help myself! I was embarrassed and did not know what to do. I did not realize it, but these were ordinary folk behaving as decent people do. And they were Christians – real ones – the like I had never seen before. They sensed what was wrong. Laurel picked up some food and handed it to me.

"Don't be frightened. You must be hungry. We won't hurt you. We'll take care of you. Tom and I have been talking about you during the night. We won't take you back and we won't let anybody else, either. We're Christians. We couldn't let you go back to that. What you've told us already is enough. If we took you back, we wouldn't be able to live with ourselves."

There was something about these people. They were kind and I felt they were telling me the truth. Maybe!

Tom told me we were only an hour's drive from Morawa and that we had come about two hundred and fifty miles overnight. We were well away from Bindoon. I started to feel safe. In an hour's time we would be three hundred miles away, only nine hours since I had made the break. Things were looking good.

It was nine o'clock and my mind went back to Bindoon and the pandemonium there.

"Spoug's gone! Hope the bastards don't find him. Good on ya, Spoug. Don't get caught!"

Keaney would be going berserk. My friends would be getting flogged. I started to cry. Laurel, God bless her, asked, "What's wrong?"

I told her and she started to cry, too. Tom could not believe it. He said, "Trust us. We will make sure you never go back there."

That was thirty six years ago and as I write this, I have a tear in my eye.

Arriving at Morawa, we went straight to the house of the Minister of the Church of Christ. He and his family made me welcome and did not look on me as a freak or a criminal. Instead, the Minister's wife cooked us a breakfast of bacon and eggs and I sat down as one of the family. But in the back of my mind, I was still waiting for the cops to come and take me away. Yet, on the other hand, I trusted these folk. They were kind and gentle.

And another miracle – the Minister's son, Jeff, had a bicycle and he let me ride it. Then, better still, he borrowed one from a friend for me.

At lunch time, I sat at the table with the two families. Afterwards, we went out to tennis. I must have stood out like a sore toe, for everyone was in white and here was I dressed in khaki shorts and shirt, a slouch hat and ex-army boots with no socks, but nobody laughed at me.

Tom and Laurel had assured me that they would get me a job with one of the farmers and not to worry, but by mid-afternoon, when nothing had happened, I became anxious.

I had better do something about a job and somewhere to stay. I had better make a move. I had to take care of myself.

With these thoughts, I quietly slipped away from the tennis and wandered into the small town to knock on doors and see if I could get a job. I had not gone far when I heard Tom's voice behind me.

"Lionel! What are you doing?"

He was concerned and hurt. Abruptly, I told him.

"Trust me", he replied. "I've almost got something organized with one of the farmers."

So I went back with him and, sure enough, as soon as the tennis was finished, he introduced me to Ken, who had a farm five miles down the road. He would give me a job at four pounds a week and my keep. What could I say? Less than twenty four hours before, I had been a slave at Bindoon, and now here I was, three hundred miles away with a paid job and somewhere to live. It was a miracle!

Ken, his wife and four children were all Christians of the Church of Christ. His wife's name was Ruth. Although they were nice people, I was scared. I was being treated as a human and it was alien to me. They spoke a language I had never heard before. They used words like, "please", "thank you" and "I beg your pardon." I was embarrassed and did not know how to cope with it. I wanted to run.

We got into the big '48 Chevvy and in ten minutes arrived at the farm. Ken showed me my sleeping quarters in a small shed next to the generating plant. He showed me how to make some bush blankets with wheat bags (woggas as they are called).

"In the morning", he said, "I will go to the Police Station and tell them you are here. Don't worry. We won't let them take you away. We just want to do it right. I know the Sergeant well and there is no way he would let you go back." His next statement let me know I was free of the tyrants. "You are sixteen and legally, they can't take you back."

I knew he was right, but I also knew the power those people had. Hadn't we been visited twice by the Commissioner of Police while I had been at Bindoon and hadn't he been announced as a good friend of Keaney and the Catholic Church?

Ken's statement reassured me, but I was far from convinced

I was safe. Also, he was a Christian and not to be trusted. I would remain on my guard and be ready to run at the slightest wrong move. I had tasted freedom and nobody would ever take it away from me. That was the promise I made to myself; I would give my life to protect it.

I was welcomed by the family and treated as one of them, particularly at the table. As I ate the evening meal with them, they asked me many questions about my background which I only half answered. There was one small reminder of what I had left and it immediately put me on my guard. These people had a black housekeeper named Winnie who did all the chores and this reminded me of the black girls at Bindoon who, like us, had been treated as slave labour. Were these Christians the same as those I had left? Were they putting on a front for me?

Winnie was seventeen years old and beautiful. I could not help but notice the lovely shape of her body and the firm breasts with the nipples that showed through her blouse. She had too, an attractive face. What was she doing as a housekeeper? Were all aboriginals treated the same by Christians? Weren't they human beings the same as us? Well, maybe this is the way it goes. The poor people are the slaves of the rich. I did not know. This was my first day in the outside world, but in time I would find out. However, I could not help feeling sorry for Winnie.

I went to bed that night in my own little 'shed room' and it felt strange not to hear the breathing and snoring of many other boys. It was a silence I had never known before. I lay awake for a long time, my mind racing. So much had happened in less than twenty four hours. It seemed too good to be true, but I did not think for one moment that the party was over and I determined to be constantly on my guard. I did not and would not trust anybody. These people seemed nice, but the people who had brought me up could be nice too when they wanted something. I fell asleep.

At six o'clock the next morning, Ken woke me. After breakfast, he wasted no time in showing me my job. It was simple. He took me out to a six hundred acre paddock that had just been ploughed. I had never in my life seen so many roots! They were so thick, I could step from one to the other. My job was to stack and burn them. He left me there with some tucker and told me he would pick me up at dark. I looked around. God, I'll be here for ever. There's millions of roots! However, I was used to hard work, so I put my head down and arse up and went for it. So what? I was free, the tucker was good and I was getting paid four quid a week. This was Monday. I had been out of Bindoon for two and a half days. So far, so good!

But at lunch time, Ken came back. "Come on, we're going to see the Police Sergeant in Morawa."

My heart sank. I looked at him and thought, "You dirty bastard, you've snitched on me." Hate welled up in me. "You cunt! I'll kill you if you betray me!"

He saw the look on my face and the hate in my eyes. He reassured me by saying, "It's O.K. I just want you to meet each other. There's nothing to worry about."

I did not trust him and was ready to run. We got to the cop shop. I was full of fear. I was introduced to the Sergeant.

All he said was, "Just behave yourself, sonny. Don't tell anyone where you're from and you'll be safe. I've heard about that place. You won't be going back there. Anyway, you're sixteen now and legally, they can't take you back."

I walked out of there the happiest boy on earth. I WAS FREE! IT COULD BE DONE! I HAD BEATEN KEANEY!

I had been on the farm nearly three months, picking and burning roots, going to the Church of Christ on Sundays and trying to mix with the family. This was the most difficult task. As hard as I tried, I could not fit in and always felt like an intruder. It was as though I suffered from a terrible inferiority complex. I always felt embarrassed when kindness or a compliment was thrown my way. It was all so strange. Quite often, I wished I was back at Boys Town, Bindoon. As harsh as that treatment had been, I had become used to it. Kindness was almost unknown to me and I became suspicious when anyone showed it to me. Either they were weak or wanted something. Ken's wife, Ruth, gave me a lot of kindness during those first three months.

Then something happened to change it all. I had, on many occasions, observed Ruth hugging and kissing her children and, at times, crying over them. This always set up a longing in me and I desperately wanted someone to hold and to hug me. I thought it would be the most precious thing in the world. So I decided what to do. Winnie lived in a caravan at the back of the house. I would go to her and ask her if she would just put her arms around me and hold me and could I do the same to her? I so desperately wanted and needed that and I was sure she would not mind if I told her. It could not do any harm.

So, late one night, I crept around and quietly knocked on the caravan door, scared, my whole body shaking. It took all the courage I had to do it.

A frightened voice came back. "Get away from here, or I'll scream!"

I needed no second telling. Frightened and embarrassed, I ran.

The next morning, Ken woke me. "When you're dressed, get down to the shed. I want to speak to you."

These words scared me. They were a direct echo from my past. Winnie must have told him. What was he going to do? He was a big man. The very tone of his voice put me on my guard. My hate for authority welled up within me. This hate took care of my fear and I knew I could take care of him, whatever he did. It gave me a sense of power and reassurance. Physically, I could take anything he dished up.

In the shed, his opening lines were, "You should be ashamed of yourself. We are a good Christian family and she is a good Christian girl. We took you in and gave you a job and a home and now you do this to us."

I had heard that song before. I had been hearing it for fourteen years – the favours people had done for me. And here it was again. I could have spewed out the hate I felt.

His next words were fatal. He did not know what he was dealing with. "Do you know what I am going to do to you for what you have done to us?" He pointed to a piece of rope lying on the floor.

I froze, not with fear, but with hate and loathing.

"I am going to pick up that rope and flog you with it."

A deadly calm that I had never known before came over me. I looked this man in the eye and said, "You may flog me if you wish. I can take that." I pointed to a rifle leaning against a post and quietly said to him, "But when you have finished flogging me, I will pick up that rifle and shoot you."

I meant it. I yelled, "You Christian bastards are all the same. You are no different to those I ran away from. You work me sixteen hours a day in the paddock picking roots and you watch from the seat of your tractor. You drag me off to Church every Sunday and display me as your fuckin' toy and now you want to flog me for something I haven't done. Now pick up the rope!"

Frightened and dismayed and, I suspect, aware for the first time that he knew nothing about me, he simply said, "You'd better leave. I'll put you on the train for Perth tonight."

I had done no wrong and this man's words condemned me. He was a mature man of the world with children of his own and he should have known enough of my background to have perceived my ignorance. Why didn't he just sit me down and talk quietly to me as a friend and explain some of the do's and dont's in the world in which I was such a complete stranger. He did not give me a chance to explain myself. I knew nothing of sex or women. I longed only to feel someone's arms around me, to make me feel human. As true as this was, he would never have believed me.

I packed the case and blankets which I had slowly bought over the three months. Ken squared up with me, my wages coming to the princely sum of five pounds.

Ruth cut me some sandwiches for the train and, with tears in her eyes, said, "You have been here for three months and not once have I seen you smile. It's very unnatural. Those people must have really hurt you. You are the best man we've ever had here as far as work goes. I will miss you and pray for you, but please make me one promise. Don't ever touch alcohol."

I said goodbye to her and Ken drove me to the station.

I arrived in Perth the next morning and knew I had to get a job and somewhere to live so I went straight to the Employment Office. I filled out the papers and handed them over the counter. The clerk looked at them and then looked at me over the top of his specs. I knew that look. He went to the phone.

"Here's trouble!" I thought. I was ready for it.

He spoke on the phone a few minutes and then came back to me. "We can't give you a job until you go and see the Child Welfare Department."

I said, "O.K. I'll go and see them."

I made my way to their office, a little apprehensive. They were "Authority" and I was not sure what they would do. But it was also a degree of defiance. I did not have to go, but I wanted to see if they would try to send me back to Bindoon. If they did, I would lead them a merry dance. I was looking for trouble and I knew it.

When I got there, I announced myself and was introduced to a man called Mr Mather. Any forebodings I may have had about these people were quickly dispelled by the grin on his face.

"You beat them, son", he said. "Good on yer! You'd better tell me all about it. The Catholic Immigration have been going off their heads. Every copper in the State has been looking for you!"

I said, "They must be blind. I've just walked down the main street of Perth with my name all over my bag and passed about eight coppers without a word."

Mr Mather smiled. "Maybe they turned a blind eye. They know about Bindoon. Anyway, you'll have to go round and see them. They can't touch you anymore. You're over sixteen. We are now your legal guardians and we have the say."

So here it was, straight from the horse's mouth. I had beaten the bastards. I was really free!

"Go and see them and ask for a Father Stinson. Then come back and we will outfit you with some clothes, get you a place to live and a job."

This was magic. These people really cared. They were on my side.!

I made my way to the Catholic Immigration Office and Stinson. I had seen this little chain-smoking slob at Boys Town a few times and had always looked upon him as a man of authority. Like all the boys, I had feared him and that fear was with me as I walked into his office. I knew he had power although I did not know how much, but I was ready for him and full of hate. He was one of them.

He recognized me instantly and with all the authority he could muster, said, "Where have you been? Brother Keaney wants you back at Bindoon to make an example of you and I'm going to send you back there."

He had lit a short fuse. Not only with what he had said, but in the degrading way he spoke. My hate and loathing for this creep and all he stood for, far outweighed any fear I may have had for him and his kind. It had been three months or more since I had been spoken to like that. I remembered, "Nobody will ever do this to me again."

With all the loathing I could muster and through gritted teeth, I said, "You take me back to Boys Town. Take me back yourself. I'll cop the terrible flogging and humiliation. You stand and watch it, if you have the guts, and when they've finished with me, Bastard, this is what I'll do. There are one hundred tough boys up there and all they need is a leader. They respect me. I will organize the biggest breakout you've ever seen. You will have one hundred to look for. How do you think you'll go? You couldn't even find me with all your powerful friends. I will tie the Brothers up, cut the phone lines and load the boys into three vehicles going in three different directions. Now, you smart bastard – take me back to Boys Town."

While I was talking, he smoked with shaking hands and turned sickly white. My hour of victory! I had waited so many years to tear one of these priests apart. I had this 'thing' where I wanted it and I relished every minute, so I continued the tirade.

"You are brave people with a strap in your hand and a doctrine for terrorizing children. You have stolen my education, told me lies, worked me like a slave, belted me for no reason, intimidated me all my life and made me live in terror. You taught me there is a hell and I believe there is, for people like you! You have a lot to answer for – all of you! If you and the likes of you are God's representatives, then I don't want a bar of Him, ever! And I swear I will never walk into a church again!"

Once again I challenged him. "Now take me back to Boys Town, you gutless bastard!"

White and trembling, he said in a shaky voice, "No, I will not send you back. You are a trouble-maker. Please leave my office and don't ever come back."

I turned with a feeling of loathing for this 'thing' that called itself a man. I had found a chink in the armour. They did not have as much power as I had thought and certainly not as individuals seen in the cold light of day and confronted on a one-to-one basis.

If there was a God, where and how did he fit in? Somebody must have created the Universe.

I went back to the Child Welfare Department and told Mr Mather what had happened.

He gave me a knowing grin and said, "They have nothing to do with you anymore. Forget about them." Then he added, "We've got you a job as an apprentice plasterer and a place to stay. Mr Farquhar will be your man and will call on you now and then to see how you are."

I stayed in Perth for a few months working as an apprentice plasterer, but I was restless and found it difficult to relate to other people. I always felt different. The other men at work had normal families and backgrounds, far removed from mine. I felt a misfit, inferior. I did not know what I wanted nor where I belonged. Nobody wanted me. So I threw in my apprenticeship and joined the Railways as a fireman. I was posted to Albany in the south of the State.

It was a big railway depot with a lot of men and boys of my age and I fitted in as best I could. I still did not trust anybody. I was always on my guard and picking up people the wrong way. I was in a strange world and had to learn how to live in it and how to cope with all the different types I met. I told few people of my background because I felt ashamed of it and it made me feel like a freak. Those I did try to tell did not believe me anyway, so I covered up the best way I could.

I met girls, went to dances and did all the things a seventeen year old would do. But I had a lot of difficulty with females. I knew nothing about them and I always thought I was ugly and that they did not want me, even though they chased me and told me I was good looking. I could not believe them. I wanted someone to love so much but was too frightened to try and did not know how to go about it, anyway. On a few occasions, the girl I was with would become so frustrated she would start to cry. I was totally naive.

My mates would tell me of their exploits with girls. They always scored. The only woman I had known had been in a brothel in Roe Street in Perth. I had gone there frightened and out of curiosity. What was wrong with me? Why couldn't I feel relaxed with girls and my friends?

Then one night before a dance, a miracle happened. One of my friends handed me a bottle of beer, saying, "Have a drink."

I did not care much for booze and until then had not even thought about it. But to fit in and be one of the boys, I took a mouthful.

The magic was instantaneous! I felt it course through my body and mind and for the first time in my life, I felt free from the turmoil, hate and pain. It was great, wonderful! I could laugh – really laugh. Where were those sheilas now? I'll screw the lot of them! This was heaven, the heaven I had been taught about. Why hadn't those Catholic bastards told me about this? This was the panacea for everything. I was happy. I fitted in with my friends. But above all, my mind and spirit had been freed. And that was after only a few mouthfuls! Give me more! Pour it in my ears or through the top of my head, I don't care. I never want to lose this feeling again. It is magic!

I had found the key and nobody would ever take it from me, not at any price! My friends gave me more and told me it was the first time they had seen me happy. A freed spirit! Half a bottle of beer later, I flaked out, though not before I had spewed the whole lot up, my head spinning and feeling sick.

So I went to the dances, the parties, the 'footie shows' and all the rest of it. I got on with the girls and found I could operate better than most of my friends, but only if I had the magic of alcohol. Without it, I was inadequate and was the frightened orphan boy. With it, I could be whoever and whatever I liked and I always made sure it was close at hand. Why not? It was my total and only security.

It was at one of the dances that I met my wife-to-be, Gladys. She was attractive and we hit it off together. After a few weeks we got engaged and made plans to get married, but it was not long before I began to have doubts. We were too young, I wasn't ready and I wanted to save some money. I told her of my feelings and naturally she was hurt and angry. I felt a heel and so as not to hurt her more, I said, "O.K. We'll get married but let's leave it for a while."

A couple of months later, the bomb fell. "I'm pregnant", she told me, crying.

We were married in November, 1955. I was half-drunk for the occasion.

My daughter, Christine, arrived a few months later. She was beautiful and I loved her dearly. Her arrival brought me closer to my wife.

I remained with the Railways for four years as a fireman on the locomotives. But the money dropped and we were finding it hard to make ends meet. When I was offered a job in the building trade, I took it, the money being much better and it gave me a chance to get back to the trade I liked. Bill, my boss, was a good tradesman. He taught me well and tutored me in the finer points of the trade. As a result, I developed into a good tradesman and found myself in demand.

After a couple of years with Bill, I went working for myself. Only twenty five, I began handling big contracts and employing men. I had the world at my feet. I was making big money. I had my own printed stationery and advertisements at the drive-in theatre.

Two more children came along – Robbie and Shaun and of course, like Christine they were beautiful and I loved them. For the first time in my life, I had something to love – my children and they gave me love, plenty of it. In time, three more arrived.

I worked hard for my family, seven days a week and up to eighteen hours a day. I loved it. I thrived on hard work. Not only was I reputed to be the best tradesman in Albany but also the quickest.

Initially, I drank only on Saturday nights with my wife and I did not touch a drop during the week. But slowly, very slowly, the pattern changed and went to Saturday night and the two 2-hourly sessions on Sunday and Sunday night. But I never touched a drop through the week as it would interfere with my work. Should I have to meet a client in a hotel, I would drink squash. This was a strict rule I made for myself – no drink during the working week.

Slowly however, my weekend binges got worse and somehow I began to drink on one or two nights during the week. It was not long before it became every night and all weekend.

When my wife complained, I would retort, "I work hard, I drink hard and I will die hard! Leave me alone!"

The contracts were getting bigger. I was drinking harder. Fear was coming into my life again, a strange fear where I did not know what I was frightened of and my body would start to shake. I shook so badly at times that at 'smokos' I had to leave the shed as I could not pick up a cup of tea in front of the men. I felt shame and remorse about this. I could not hold a level steady or scale a plan with my rule and found it difficult to concentrate. I was now working under tremendous mental pressure. At times, my wife and also some of my good friends would comment on my large consumption of alcohol. This would cut me to the bone and I would tell them to mind their own business.

Many people remarked, "You are a top tradesman but you drink too much. Why don't you cut it down?"

I would always reply, "Just leave me alone."

I had had fourteen years of people telling me what to do and running my life and nobody was going to do that anymore. Nobody! I would run my life my way, at any cost and whatever the consequences. I would cop them sweet. And anyhow, I can stop drinking whenever I want – I just don't want to. I'm not going to throw away the only thing I've found to be my comfort and panacea in all situations. Alcohol had become the answer to everything.

Now there were six children, all beautiful and dear to me and we lived in a brick home that I had built. We were proud of it. My children gave me plenty of love. I would come home from the pub, half-drunk and the six of them would crawl all over me. But I would be tired and the ulcer that would develop in my stomach was beginning to give me a hard time. Although I loved my kids, because of my physical and mental state I could not return their love as much as I wanted to and I would gently push them away. I felt guilty. I was their dad but, as much as I wanted to, I found it difficult to show my love.

I was then thirty years old and my drinking had got right out of hand. There was not a night I did not come home drunk and fall asleep without eating. First thing in the morning, I cracked a bottle of booze and then left for work without breakfast. Somehow, I had to get through to lunch time and then down to the pub so that I could get through the afternoon and then straight back to the pub after work. This had become the routine. By now, I could not function without the booze.

Contracts started to drop off, my men started to leave me and my work efficiency was suffering. But strangely enough, I honestly did not know why! The bills were mounting up, jobs were not completed and my fears were getting worse. I was not a father to my children or a husband to my wife. I was no longer the best tradesman in town and I was becoming a 'has-been' and a laughing stock. My friends, in despair, pleaded with me, but to no avail.

"Go to hell!" I would tell them. "It has nothing to do with you! Go and take care of your own family."

Eventually, I lost all my contracts and was back on wages. I sold all my gear, scaffolding, barrows, mixers, planks – the lot – and it all went down my throat.

I had to send myself bankrupt to get the creditors off my back. My wife took bankruptcy very hard. Everybody in town knew about it and it brought shame on her and my children. Me? I just got drunk and didn't come home!

My whole being was riddled with fear. I became frightened of everything and everybody. My world was crumbling and I blamed everybody and everything but the booze. I went to ministers of religion and (yes!) even Catholic priests.

People told me I was an alcoholic – the ultimate ignominy. I smacked one man in the mouth for his insulting comment. I couldn't be an alcoholic! I wasn't one of them. If only the builders would get off my back, my creditors give me a little more time to pay, my wife leave me alone, my ulcer stop hurting ... it couldn't be alcohol. Something in a bottle couldn't do this. The thought was absurd. It had to be something else.

The drinking went on despite the pleas of my friends. I could no longer go to work and support my family. The guilt and remorse were unbearable and I had to continue drinking to stop the torment in my head. Blackouts had become an everyday occurrence. I could not remember anything from the night before or about my drinking bouts and the fear of not knowing what I had said or done in these periods of amnesia was becoming frightening.

Finally, at the age of thirty two, my wife asked me to leave. I was stunned! Was this really happening? It seemed like a nightmare. What about my kids? I didn't want to leave them.

Who would take care of them? My wife assured me that they would be taken care of and that she just wanted me to leave.

She packed my bags. The children thought I was going to a bush job as I had done many times in the past and I just let them believe it. They asked me how long I would be gone.

Holding back the tears, I said, "For a long time. I don't know when I'll be back. Be good kids for Mum."

But leaving was not easy. I had lost my children who, until now, were the only ones I had ever really loved. Now they were gone. My life was smashed. There was nothing left. No worse tragedy could befall me. I was left hanging in despair. Nothing mattered any more.

Why had this happened? The God I had been taught about must be a tyrant! An old man with a big stick and a big book who seemed hell-bent on punishment for the slightest fault.

It did not add up. I thought, "Had I been so bad in the first two years of my life to warrant what had already happened to me? If there was any justice, surely I should be square with Him by now for whatever it was I had done."

I decided what I would do. I would write to my sister, Maureen. She lived in Adelaide. I would start a brand new life. There was still a small flame of hope left. All was not lost. Of course, it had all been a mistake. From now on, things would be different.

I caught the train for Perth that night, drunk. I was lost but still with a glimmer of hope.

CHAPTER

4

> We, who live in prison and in whose lives
> there is no event but sorrow, have to measure
> time by throbs of pain and the record of bitter
> moments.
> Suffering, as curious as it may sound to you,
> is the means by which we exist.
> Suffering in the past is necessary for our
> continued identity.
>
> Oscar Wilde

The next morning I arrived in Perth, as full as a boot and no recollection of the scenic journey so often advertised.

As a member of the Buffalo Lodge, I went straight to a boarding house they ran and in a semi-drunken stupor, wrote a letter to my sister. In thirty two years, I had seen her only once. Discovering that she, too, had been brought to Australia under the Catholic Migration Scheme, I had, in more affluent days, brought her to Perth for a holiday. Now I was lucky to still have her address.

I got a job in Perth laying bricks, doing it hard and always suffering from the effects of booze. A couple of weeks had gone by when a letter arrived from Maureen.

"Come over here to us and start a new life. Get a good woman and start again."

At last. Here was the break I had been waiting for. I would go to South Australia and begin a new life, leaving the past behind me. I wouldn't have to drink any more. All my worries would be gone.

With these thoughts in mind, I boarded the train for Adelaide. On the trip across, though drunk all the time, my feelings were much the same as when I left England and again, when I was walking down the road from Bindoon in the middle of the night.

"At last I'm free. This time it will be different."

Maureen, her husband Jeff and their children met me at the station. They were excited and dressed up, waiting for His Majesty to step off the train. And three parts drunk, in my best suitcase-wrinkled clothes, I fell off the train at their feet.

I got up and said, "I'm not used to these new shoes yet. They hurt my feet."

I had bought the 'new' shoes at St. Vincent de Paul's for two bob and they had a hole in the sole which, I hoped, they had not seen when I fell over.

This was the introduction to my new family and my brand new life. I dragged Jeff, who, it turned out, had been brought up in cotton wool, into the first bar we came across, to celebrate the arrival of the hero. He was not impressed as he watched me swallow four beers to his one. I probably drank more in that first half-hour with him than he would drink in a year. He kept reminding me that Maureen and the kids were out in the car, that she had cooked a special meal for the occasion and that they wanted to talk to me.

"She hasn't seen you for so many years, and that was only once, and the kids want to talk to their uncle. Let's go home."

I knew that what he was saying was right and I felt guilty, but I did not want to leave that bar. I eventually did, but not without a cargo of booze. Jeff shook his head. He could not understand why I had to take so much home with me.

Being my sister, Maureen made allowances to the family for my drinking. "He's just lost his family. It's been a long trip for him. He is under extreme pressure. He'll be alright in a couple of days."

I thought, "Sis, you are dead right."

I sat at the table to a lovely meal, three sheets to the wind, trying to hold myself together. I wasn't hungry. I never was when I drank. But I had to try to eat this meal, to please my sister. That is all I remember.

The next morning, I was full of shame, remorse and fear.

What had I done? What had I said? Maureen told me that I had flaked out, fallen forward and my face had landed in the meal. Jeff, as horrified as she was, lifted my head out of the roast. Full of shame, she had looked across the table at the face covered in mashed potato, peas and gravy and thought, "Enter the Hero, my long lost brother!"

I promised them I would not drink so much. I told them that nothing like this had ever happened to me before. Of course, it was a lie. I was becoming tired of hearing myself repeating the same stories to cover up my drinking and subsequent behaviour. It was contrary to my basic nature to lie like this. And to my own family! The loss of my children must be driving me mad. I knew that somehow I had to control my drinking while at Maureen's. I did not want to subject her to another embarrassing scene like the one which had occurred the previous evening. She had told her husband and children what a great guy and brilliant tradesman I was. And yet her brother, the only member of her family and who she had hoped to look up to and admire, had, on his first night in her home, humiliated her.

By this time, bed wetting had become common practice. It often happened when I got drunk. My sister was meticulously clean and I dare not wet the bed. For her, that would have been the ultimate ignominy. At all costs, I had to control my drinking and under terrible mental agony, I did.

I got a job with an Adelaide brick firm. I started with a new set of tools which Jeff bought me as I had sold mine. For two weeks, things went well. I went straight home from work with two bottles of beer, one for before tea and one after. But it was hell. Never in the past had I tried controlled drinking and I knew, sooner or later, I would get drunk again. But I dared not do so at Maureen's.

Then the inevitable happened. I came home late one night, very drunk, when I knew the house would be asleep. I went to bed, reminding myself, at all costs, not to wet the bed. I fell asleep and started to dream. I wanted to go to the toilet but I could not get out – the glass door to my room had no inside handle – I was trapped but I had to get out so I put my fist through the glass door. The noise of the shattering glass woke me. I had put my fist through the bedroom window!

The next morning, Maureen gave it to me! Ashamed and full of self-loathing, I told her I would get out. She asked me to go anyway.

I was lucky that the firm was doing a job at Port Augusta, about two hundred miles away. The firm booked me into a hotel which was right up my alley! I stayed there for two weeks and somehow managed to work every day with the aid of drink. I had learned the art of getting booze to work without being detected. I could not work without booze and had to earn the money to buy it so that I could cope.

On this fine line, I was able to work, though not without great difficulty. I was restless and wanted to move on, where to did not matter. I just wanted to run. It was a relief when I got the chance to go to Darwin with three other brickies.

Darwin was an alkie's paradise! Everybody drank – at work, in the streets, anywhere and everywhere. But they did not all drink like me or for the reasons I drank. I had to take it to work, otherwise, no work! Without it, I was non-functional. Full stop!

The small team I was with worked on a small brick cottage on the other side of Darwin Harbour. The other brickies, hard drinkers as they were and good blokes too, knew I drank differently to them. They respected me as a tradesman and tried to help me.

"You're a top tradesman, Geordie, but you drink too much. If you don't cut it down, we'll have to find someone else and we don't want to do that. We like you. Just cut down the drink a bit and you'll be O.K."

But always the defiance. "Fuck you. Mind your own business and don't tell me how to run my life."

Soon, I was no longer required. I had never been sacked as a tradesman and the experience was painful and humiliating.

I flew back to Darwin with $700 burning a hole in my pocket. In 1968, that was a lot of money. I booked into a hotel. Within two or three days my money was gone. I was flat broke and in the D.Ts. I was terrified, in a strange city and I did not know anyone. But I knew I had to get off the booze and straighten myself out. I found a small beach near the town where there was a water tap. For the first time, I went through the cruel process of drying out, cold turkey. It was agony – three days of sweating it out and drinking only water. I ate nothing. The shakes finally settled down sufficiently for me to be able to at least walk down the street, without too much fear, to see if I could start again.

My children were constantly with me, the task of keeping them out of my head impossible without booze. With it, it was bearable; without it, impossible. I was trapped by my feelings and felt I would go insane. Where had gone the courage of only yesterday that had enabled me to cope with fourteen years of suffering? I will muster it up again; straighten myself out and go back to my family and try again. Of course, that is what I will do!

I rang Carol, my sister-in-law in Western Australia to get my wife to the phone, but she would not come. Nor would she allow any of my children to speak to me. With this news, I despaired. With it went all my good intentions of trying again.

I got a job laying bricks on a three-storied building. All went well for a week or two before I started drinking again. Before long, I was back on the tightrope, drinking just enough to function with a degree of normality and bear the heights of the scaffolding I was working on.

But one day, I got caught. I was on a scaffold with another brickie, constructing a wall above a concrete stair-well. We had almost finished when I turned round to pick up some mud from my mortar board and as I turned to face the wall again, it was coming towards me! The wind had caught it, rocked it and it was swaying towards me. All I could do was to brace myself and lean against it so that it would not carry me down to the bottom. But I was no match for the weight of the six hundred cement bricks. I went down with it, to land on the concrete stair-well fifteen feet below.

I did not feel the impact and, stunned, I freed myself from beneath the pile of bricks and mortar. I sat on the stairs, blood pouring from my head. Men came running from everywhere.

"Give me a smoke. I'll be O.K." The blood dripped on to my hands and ran down my fingers on to the cigarette.

"Come on! We're taking you to hospital."

My immediate thought was, "No way! I can't get a drink in there. I'll go crazy. I'm not going." And I told them so.

With blood running down my face and into my eyes I knew that I needed a doctor, but the fear of no drink in a hospital terrified me. Then the agonising pain of the fall entered my head, neck and shoulders and with it came an ounce of sanity. With pain like this, I needed help.

Relieved, the men took me to the Darwin Hospital where a Chinese doctor put thirteen stitches in my scalp.

He said, "We will have to keep you here for at least two weeks. By some miracle, nothing has been broken, but there could be serious repercussions."

I could bear the physical pain no matter how excruciating, but not the mental torment. I had to have a drink to stop it. Still half stunned and unable to move my neck and shoulders, I bolted for the nearest pub and, in doing so, automatically put an end to any insurance claim. I was penniless.

I had to have a drink. It forced me into 'cold biting' people – begging. The shame of this did not help my already tormented mind. Food I didn't need and smokes I could find in the way of butts wherever people threw them, no matter where – even on the floors of public toilets. Clothes did not matter either – shorts and shirt, or even just shorts were the accepted way of Darwin life. And nature provided a bed anywhere I liked. All I needed and all that mattered was alcohol, in any shape or form.

I bummed around the Darwin streets and pubs, still in physical pain. I had to be careful who I asked for money as they were a wild lot and would fight at the drop of a hat.

One day, I saw how they fought. For the first time, in horror, I saw a man kick another while he lay helpless on the ground. At the time I was unaware that I was standing at the doorway to a horrible, cruel world in which I would be trapped for a long time. In my bumming around, I ran into my own type, people of the same mental calibre and caught in the same web.

Paul and Keith were crocodile hunters who lived on their small boat, but never went hunting. They were only interested in drinking. It followed – I lived on the boat with them.

In Darwin, at the time, there were a number of Japanese

fishing trawlers and my two new friends were able to go aboard these ships, seemingly at will, and I went with them. The Japanese seamen were polite. They made us welcome and gave us food and saki to drink. They took our dirty clothes and insisted that we get in to the canvas bath tub on the deck.

It was during one of these visits, the three of us three parts full of saki, that we decided that, instead of using the canvas bath we would dive overboard and bathe in the ocean. We jumped in from the main deck, twenty feet above water.

When I hit the water, I panicked. I realized how weak I was and that I would not have the strength to keep afloat. Paul and Keith, who had pulled themselves back aboard via a mooring rope, watched me floundering about in the water, unaware of my fear. They evidently thought I was playing a game. Frightened, I called to them, knowing that if I did not get help quickly I would drown. Then I realized that, like me, they were drunk on saki and may not see, until it was too late, that I was in serious trouble.

Gripped by fear and having no control over my mind, I started to go under. I was gone. With a supreme effort, I raised my head above water again. It was then that they realized I was in trouble and, instantaneously, they dived over the side. I cried with relief. They were strong men and with encouragement and kind words they got me back on board.

Luck or fate? Twice, within months, I had looked Death in the face.

There were times in Darwin when, because of lack of money and my physical and mental inability to procure it, I was forced to endure the nightmare of drying out 'cold turkey'. I had no idea that there were places and people who could help me through the horrendous ordeal. Mentally, I was cut off from the world and I was consumed by self-loathing. There could not be anyone else on earth who drank the way I did. Who would understand? And so I carried the burden alone.

By this time, my body would shake uncontrollably and my legs would not support even my light weight, so that, without a drink I walked like a drunken man. Co-ordination was a painful effort and every fibre of my being cried out for alcohol.

I was this way walking around Darwin one morning. It was

the Wet Season. The sky was as black as pitch and weighing down on me like a heavy blanket of doom. I looked across the harbour. There was a storm coming. The clouds appeared blacker and heavier than the sky and I imagined them carrying sheets of rain powerful enough to dissolve me where I stood. This thought gripped me with terror and awe. It made my body shake but it was only the beginning of the magnitude of my terror.

The rumbling thunder came, muffled at first, like a dampened drum. Then slowly, like a universal orchestra reaching a crescendo, it made a sound that would surely smash the heavens – so loud and frightening its very vibrations shook me. And as though it had not terrified me enough, it completed the display of awesome power with bolts of lightning, the like of which I had never seen before. The scenario finished with a mighty crack of a whip that lashed the universe. I shook as never before. The sweat poured down my face. In panic, I ran inside a shed, but it was worse. The rain hammered down on the iron roof as though I was in a jam tin and I could not escape the noise. I would go mad if it did not stop. I prayed like a helpless child, the tears of emotion pouring down my face. I had experienced many types of loneliness and fear, but nothing like this . I felt like a fish terrified of water. The storm raged on for perhaps another half hour whilst I fought desperately for my sanity.

On another occasion in Darwin, I was sick and weak and shaking so violently that I could not get the top off the bottle and, in this state, broke it. I had no money to buy another. Knowing full well that if I was seen like this, I would be put in a straight jacket and locked away, I ran into a public toilet to hide and try to pull myself together. I looked in the mirror and I could not believe what I saw looking back at me! The face was contorted but it was the eyes! They were the eyes of a madman, a terrified madman! I was appalled. It couldn't be me looking back at me, but some ugly demon! I ran like a petrified rabbit and crawled under a house where nobody could see me. I stayed there until dark.

I had come to Darwin in April of that year during the 'Dry' when, though very hot, the conditions are bearable. Then came October – the beginning of 'The Wet' when the humidity is stifling and the atmosphere takes on an air of terrible depression. I learned from the locals that the suicide rate at that time of the year is high. A lot of people go South during 'The Wet', particularly those not accustomed to the tropics. To remain, one took the risk of going 'troppo'.

So that's what was wrong with me! If I went South, everything would be O.K. Of course! It was easy to say, but how was I going to get the plane fare? It was becoming harder to work. How would I save the $120 needed for the fare? A seemingly impossible task, but an inner voice told me that I must get out or go insane. I had worked with and spoken to many men in the same predicament. They had been trying for years to save the fare out of Darwin but had found it impossible and would probably die there.

Then it all came back to me. I had got out of Bindoon against seemingly impossible odds. I could do it again, although it would be a hundred times harder. Hadn't I already had two close shaves with death in Darwin? And many times been at the door of insanity? I should not tempt Fate any more.

Perhaps it was Fate that organized an incident which told me, without a shadow of doubt, that I must flee this place. I was stacking cement on contract with Brian, a man I had worked with before. We had knocked off, had a few beers and were returning to the shack where we camped when a car pulled up.

"You want a lift, boys?"

They were two white fellows we had spoken to in the pub. We hopped in. They started to tell us about a fight they had just had in the hotel where both of them had beaten up a black fellow and then taken off.

I was not impressed. Two on to one was not fair and they were bragging about it! We pulled up and for some reason I turned round and peered out of the back window. A taxi had pulled up behind us. The occupants, five big, angry Thursday Islanders were getting out of the cab as though they meant business. I knew it meant trouble – big trouble! And instinctively I knew that they were friends of the man these two had beaten up. And I wasn't wrong. But there was no fear in me. I was no part of it, so I turned round and said quietly, "We're in for it."

The two responsible turned white. Brian said to me, "Don't

get out of the car, whatever you do."

I had done nothing wrong and had nothing to fear. I got out of the car. Before I got a chance to do anything, I was surrounded by five big Thursday Islanders. They attacked me from all sides and the only thing I remember is saying to myself, "Geordie, whatever happens, don't go down on the ground. If you do, you'll be kicked to death."

I pleaded with those men. I realized they had the wrong man; that the driver of the car looked similar to me and I kept calling out, "You have got the wrong person", but they didn't take any notice. They kept beating and kicking me.

Suddenly they stopped and turned their attention to the car. In this short respite, I took off. My face was bloodied, my eyes were swollen and closing, my mouth smashed, my nose spread across my face and the rest of my body hurting, but I was glad to have escaped.

Back at the hotel, my friends gave me a drink, asked me what had happened and who was responsible. They wanted to retaliate, but I said, "No!"

Lucky to have escaped, I did not want another confrontation. They also offered to hospitalize me, which, in the condition I was in, I should have been, but I refused. Once again, the thought that in hospital, I would not be able to get a drink, horrified me.

I had to get out of Darwin or be killed or go insane. But how was I to get the fare? If I worked I drank my wage. If I drank, I didn't get work.

By a coincidence, I heard of a man called Silver who lived in a small caravan on his own and somehow had managed to get off the booze and straighten himself out. I wondered if he could help me. I went to see him.

Silver seemed to understand. He helped me to dry out and gave me some food. Then I was able to get a small contract which involved laying about five thousand bricks and I knew, if I could stick to this contract and either control my drinking or not drink at all, I would soon have my fare out of that hell. There was no choice.

So I set to work. It was impossible to leave booze alone. Without it, I shook, could not think and knew I could not function as a tradesman. So I compromised with myself. I would take a bottle of rum to work in my bag and, through the day, occasionally give myself a charge to keep me on an even mental keel. Also, I was working on high scaffolding and feared falling. It was difficult, but I knew that it had to be done. At times like this, I appreciated my hard upbringing. It had given me the determination to go through with this.

I soon had the $120 fare to Sydney where there was a job and a home waiting for me with one of my ex-Bindoon friends, Joe Norman. I went straight to the airline office and purchased the ticket before I had the chance to drink away the money. I gave the ticket to my friend, Silver and asked him to hold it and not to give it back under any circumstances and to make sure that, when the time came, I got on the plane. I stayed in Darwin for another five days, working, in order to have some spending money for when I got to Sydney.

The big day arrived and, until then, I had not got drunk. But four hours before I was to board the plane, I became terrified. I got drunk, really drunk, but true to his word, Silver got me to the Airport and poured me on to the plane. I remember nothing of the trip except that we had to change planes in Adelaide and that a kind air hostess directed me to the flight to Sydney.

When I got to Mascot, Joe Norman was waiting for me. He took me straight to an R.S.L. Club. He wanted to show me the poker machines. It suited me down to the ground because I could get a drink. We stayed there for a while and then Joe took me home and introduced me to his wife and three children. He showed me the little flat attached to the house and told me I could start work next day.

He knew nothing of my drinking habits and had no idea what he was letting himself in for. This made me feel like a criminal and a cheat. How was I going to cover up my drinking? How was I going to function on the job? I knew Joe was a fast bricklayer and he would expect me to be as quick as he was and I also knew, without a shadow of doubt, that those days had gone and it would take all my energy, stamina and mental ability to keep pace with him. This added to the fears I already felt. But here was a chance to start again. This time it would be different. I had a friend. I had a little flat. I had a job.

Everything was going for me. I would control my drinking and start a new life.

I had been working for Joe under duress, for about three months. The new life I had promised myself was not happening. My lifestyle was becoming worse, my drinking increasing again and my fears growing. I missed days at work because I shook so. I could not control my tools, but I knew that if I could get a drink before work I would be O.K. This was difficult because I lived virtually in the same house as Joe and how was I going to get the booze in the car? If I could get it to work, how was I going to drink it on the job without him seeing me? This was a dilemma. I had to find a way to get it to work and it did not take me long. At night, when I knocked off, I would go to the pub and buy six bottles. When it was dark, I would open Joe's car and plant two bottles of beer firmly under the passenger's seat, taking care that they would not rattle. Knowing that I had booze with me, I would be confident enough to go to work in the morning.

But Joe was no fool. He could see what was happening to me and on several occasions, suggested I try to cut down my drinking. I told him drinking was not responsible for my behaviour – it was the loss of my family.

Joe said to me, with great concern, "Spoug, I hate to tell you this, but you are an alcoholic."

The word alcoholic repulsed me. He could call me anything, but not that.

Then he went on to say, "I've seen men like you in the Army who finished up in the gutter, drinking metho and sleeping in the parks."

I laughed and said, "You are joking, Joe. I'll blow my brains out before I come to that."

He said, "We'll see."

We came home from work one day and Joe said, "We are going back to Western Australia. Do you want to come?"

Immediately fear gripped me. I had travelled the Nullarbor before by train. It had been a long journey and I could not have made it without booze. Joe had a wife and children. He needed me to help him with the driving and I was certain he would not let me drink or take drink in the car.

I said, "I don't know, Joe. I'd like to go with you." I thought for a moment while he waited for my answer. "I'll go with you on one condition", I continued. "You put twelve bottles of beer in the boot and keep twelve bottles there all the way."

He replied, "But you'll get drunk and won't be able to drive!"

"I promise I won't get drunk", I told him, "but I can't drive without a drink. My nerves will not stand it and if you attempt to stop me from drinking – I don't care where we are, in the middle of the Nullarbor or anywhere else – I will get out of the car and leave you. I mean it."

He agreed. These conditions may sound hard but they had to be. I knew the fear and torment of drying out and I was not going to do it in the middle of the Nullarbor in a locked car with my friend and his family. I also knew that Joe realized my conditions had to be fulfilled.

We drove over without incident; no spare wheel; no spanners, but we made it back to Perth.

Two years had passed since I had seen my family. My immediate reaction was to go and see my children. I was overwhelmed by nostalgia. The next morning I caught the train for Albany, my home town, and arrived at seven o'clock in the morning. I was in far worse condition than when I had left. Then they had not wanted to know me. What would it be like now?

I arrived at the railway station with two cans of beer in my bag. I knew I could not face my family the way I was. To stop the shakes I would have to consume enough alcohol to make me half drunk and I could not go and see my children in that state.

Then I recalled the words of a friend many years before. He had said to me in a bar, "Geordie, if ever you get into trouble with alcohol, go and see my mother."

Her name was Mrs Atkins. It was strange that, at this time, I should remember those words as I stood on the platform in my present dilemma. I wandered off to a quiet park and sat on a seat and thought about it.

I was thirty four years of age. Should I go and see Mrs Atkins? She was a well known identity in the town – a good Catholic, as hard as nails and a staunch football supporter. She went to extremes in the support of her team, so much so that her umbrella was red and white as was the little tent she set up on the side of the oval. Should any opposition standing close by make disparaging remarks about her team, she would thrash them with the umbrella. This was the lady I was going to see!

Because it was a small town, I was sure she would know what had happened to my family. Would she condemn me for not supporting them? Would she give me an ear bashing? These questions raced through my head. The last thing I needed at that moment was to be chastised by an old bag! But I had no choice.

I drank the two cans of beer. They may as well have been water for they had no effect on me whatever. Then summoning up my courage, I slowly made my way up the steep hill to Annie Atkins's house. I arrived in a scared condition and knocked on her door.

Annie came to the door. She asked, "What's wrong, son?" The very tone of her voice soothed me.

I said, "Mrs Atkins, I think I have a problem with drink."

She spoke with compassion. "Come in, son."

She sat me down at the kitchen table. I held the table to stop my hands shaking and pressed my feet against the floor to stop my legs shaking, but I could not stop sweating.

Annie said, "You're very sick, aren't you son?"

That stunned me. I hadn't told her I was sick. How did she know? She made some tea, only half filling the big mug.

She said, "If I fill it, you'll spill it everywhere, you're shaking so much."

I could not even lift the mug off the table. She came across and raised it to my lips, saying, "You are in a bad way."

I was still waiting for the blast. She would settle me down and then tear strips off me for my behaviour over the last two years. But she didn't.

She gave me some tablets to take with the tea, saying, "These will calm you. I can't help you much because I'm not an alcoholic, but I'll ring up and introduce you to a member of Alcoholics Anonymous."

This statement shook me. Was I that bad? Did I need to go where all the bums went? Annie told me that her husband had been an alcoholic and that he had got to the state that I was now in – and worse – and through his behaviour, she had learned about the disease. She understood my dilemma and assured me that something could be done.

She rang a member of A.A. who came round immediately. His name was Ginger. Here again, I expected to have strips torn off me. Instead, he sat me down and I could feel the love and understanding from him. I felt an affinity with him. He was not a stranger. He told me about his own life; what had happened to him; what booze had done to him and as he related his story, I was able to identify with a lot of my life and the progression of my drinking. It seemed as though he had been reading my mail!

He explained to me that because I was an alcoholic, my physical make-up was different to 'normal' people. That once I took a drink of alcohol, it set up a chemical reaction within me, over which I had no control; that willpower had nothing to do with it. If you like, an allergy to alcohol. He explained that it took only one mouthful to trigger off this chemical mechanism and as soon as I instigated it, I was powerless and condemned to drink against my will.

This astounded me because it answered so many questions. Why I couldn't drink like my workmates and other normal people, when on so many occasions I had promised my wife that I would have a couple of beers after work and then go home.

I could never fathom out why or how my workmates and my friends could walk into a bar, have two beers and then go home. Despite promises to myself and my family, I was always there at closing time to be swept out with the butts. This one statement, that I was allergic to alcohol, answered so many questions.

Ginger went on to tell me about the disease and that all that was wrong with me was that I was allergic to alcohol. It seemed too simple. There had to be more to it than this. I found it difficult to believe him. But he went on to tell me about the progression of the disease of alcoholism. That, like any disease, if not treated, it would become worse. He explained that the disease was a three-fold one – spiritual, physical and mental. He assured me that there was hope. If I did not pick up one drink, one day at a time, I could recover from this dilemma and lead a normal life.

I knew this man had an answer for me. I felt at ease with him. Not once did he point the finger at me.

He said, " I'll take you to an A.A. meeting where you will hear stories of people who were in the same dilemma as you. There's hope for you. We can help you, but it's up to you."

I was in a shocking state of withdrawal. He gave me some tablets, some material to read, found me a place to live and offered me the use of his kitchen any time I wished to sit on my own with a pot of tea and listen to tapes of stories of other alcoholics.

I did not have a drink for a week. Then I went to see my family. I was very nervous. I did not know what would be said or how my children would react.

Belinda, my youngest daughter, was five years old. She saw me coming and raced down the footpath, yelling, "Daddy! Daddy! You've come home!"

She jumped into my arms. I tried to hide my tears. I felt ashamed. I hadn't supported them for two years and in the house, I felt like a stranger.

I spoke to my wife about the chances of a reconciliation for the sake of the children.

"You stay sober for twelve months and I'll think about it."

It seemed hopeless. It was a promise I could not make. It was like a death sentence hanging over me.

I stayed in Albany for three months and during that time, attended meetings of A.A. Always on the table was a little sign – SOMEBODY CARES. Those two words shook me. Who would care about me? I felt like a leper. I hadn't looked after my family, I had walked out of that town owing a lot of money and I had abused and hurt a lot of people. There could not be another person on the earth who had done the things I had done and I wanted to run.

But I listened to the stories of other alcoholics and was amazed and relieved that there were other people, just like me, who had done the things I had done, some of them even worse. I felt an affinity with these people. I felt comfortable with them. They were my own kind.

The members of A.A. spent a lot of time with me, but there were periods when I was confused and irritated. Hanging on the wall at every meeting were the twelve steps of A.A. and in two or three of them, the word God appeared. I knew these people had an answer, but here it was again. With that one word, GOD, memories of the past came surging back. I could never forgive God for what He had done.

At this stage of my life, I had come to the conclusion that God was an invention of Catholicism. An invention to dominate people's lives with fear. I had rejected this concept years before and here I was confronted by a mob of religious cranks. At the initial meetings, they had not spoken of God and I became suspicious. These people were clever. They were going to suck me in and, at the appropriate time, would introduce me to the hymn book and bible. First, I expected to see the organ in the corner, then, a couple of meetings later, the collection plate, the hymn book and finally, when they had gained my confidence, they would introduce the man with the back-to-front collar. But it did not happen.

They strongly suggested that I stay away from my family because I was not ready to cope with that sort of emotional stress. I thought they were being harsh. I had missed my children for two years. I had come home especially to see them and for a reconciliation with my wife and they were telling me to stay away. I found this difficult to accept.

I had been sober for five weeks. The trauma this created was enough in itself and now they were giving me another burden – to stay away from my children, the thing that I wanted most. It was painful and I knew I could not manage it.

It was only a matter of time before I picked up a drink. I do not know how many days I drank but I do know that it was the members of A.A. who took me to hospital to be dried out – the first of many occasions I was to be hospitalized as a result of alcoholism.

After drying out, I visited my wife again and suggested a reconciliation. Again, she put a twelve month trial on me. I knew it was impossible and that I would have to leave Albany. The tears I cried that day really hurt. I knew that while I continued to drink I would never get my children back. But I just didn't know how to stop and I felt worthless.

I decided to hitch-hike back to Sydney. I got as far as Perth and landed in a flop house – a 'snore' with other people like me. There I met a man who was in the same situation as I was. He was finding it difficult to raise the train fare back to Sydney. He told me where we could get a job on a saw mill in the South-west. Although the wages were not high, we could get the fare to Sydney if we could stay off the booze long enough.

We found our way to the saw mill, about 200 miles from Perth. We arrived drunk, penniless and with only the clothes we stood up in. I set to work on a job alien to me – tailing out on a circular saw. It terrified me, mainly because my nerves were shot to pieces. But I knew I had to persevere. The work was hard and by now, the pain of my ulcer was nearly killing me. But with the tenacity I was born with or which had been bashed into me, I stuck to it.

The life was harsh, the wages meagre and the prospect of leaving that mill remote because I could not stop drinking. I struggled along most of the time without food because I spent the money on booze. The guy in the next hut had a little vegetable garden and for some time, my friend and I lived on potatoes and spinach, which we stole from his garden.

There seemed only one way out. In this mill, men were given the opportunity to work double shifts which entailed doing the eight hour shift from 7.30 a.m. to 3.30 p.m., then having a half hour break before returning to work. I knew I had to work these double shifts, but undernourished and suffering from alcoholism, I wondered if I could stand up to it. I just had to!

Many of the men who worked the double shift could not last the distance. They were big and strong and used to the work. I decided I would try. If I didn't, I would rot in this timber mill.

With unbearable stomach pains, I made the effort. The foreman was always looking for the quitter and I was not going to be one of them. About halfway through, the stomach pains increased and my back was burning, but I battled on. The shift was to finish at midnight, but by eleven o'clock it became too much for me. In the toilet I doubled up in agony, realizing I could not go on. In spite of my pride and my unwillingness to give the foreman the satisfaction of seeing me quit, I knew I was beaten.

He looked at me with a sly grin. "Another quitter!"

I knew it was pointless to explain so I went back to my hut. By my bed were six cans of beer which I had left there for the end of the shift and, normally, alcohol would relieve the pains in my stomach. I lay in bed and drank a can of beer but it did not ease the pain. Tired, I fell asleep. When I woke the next morning, the pain was still there. There were five cans of beer still beside my bed. I drank one but it did not ease the pain and I knew that something serious was wrong. I recalled that on past occasions, if after a drink, I stuck my fingers down my throat and spewed up, the pain would diminish, so I struggled down to the water tank to fill myself up with water until I had to throw it up. Now, the pain was excruciating and I felt weak. I drank some water, stuck my fingers down my throat but nothing happened!

I sat down on the step of the hut in agony. Fortunately, two men spotted me. One of them asked, "Are you O.K.?"

I nodded.

They walked away and then one turned round and came back to me. He said, "You're sick, aren't you? We'd better take you to the hospital."

They carried me to a car and took me the five miles to the Manjimup Hospital. They were carrying me to the entrance when a doctor saw me through the glass doors. He came out and said to the men, "Bring him straight in here."

I was on the verge of collapse. The doctor examined me, had me X-rayed and announced, "We have to operate immediately. You have two hours to live!"

I returned from the operating theatre with a tube up my nose and down my throat. I knew I had to get out to get a drink. I pulled the tube out of my nose. Fortunately, a nurse saw me.

She hurried over and said, "You will die without that tube down your throat! Your stomach is filled with poison after the operation. You have poisoned your whole system and we have to pump it out of your stomach."

I understood this, and it was with much pain and coaxing by the nurse that I was able to swallow the tube again. At that stage, I was not too fussed about dying.

I stayed in hospital for an agonising ten days, always wanting to run to the pub, but somehow, I stayed there. With the scar on my stomach still not healed, I convinced the doctor that I was ready to go and immediately went to the pub, despite the doctor's warning.

I went back to the saw mill and told the manager I was ready to start.

He looked at me. "No way", he said. "You won't be fit for at least three months."

How could I stay in one of those huts all day with no money or booze? I would go insane. I could not leave the place because I had no money. I was trapped.

I said to him, "I want to start work on Monday."

He looked at me and said, "O.K. Geordie. You can try but we will not be responsible."

On Monday, I saw the foreman. He was of the same opinion as the manager – that I was insane, but he apologised for sneering at me when I had been unable to finish the double shift.

He said, "With the guts you've got, I think you can start work."

I worked the whole day and despite the doctor's warnings, I got drunk that night and remained that way for a long time. Jack and I scraped enough money together to begin our hitch-hike to Sydney. He drank a lot, but not the way I did.

Several times he said to me, "If you don't cut down, we are not going to get to Sydney."

We got on the road, getting as far as Southern Cross, about 400 miles from Manjimup. How we got there I will never know. One of the few things I do remember is waking up with Jack in an orchard, covered in frost. It was a wonder we did not freeze to death. When we landed in Southern Cross, I sensed that Jack was going to leave me. He did. He gave me the slip.

My first night in Southern Cross was freezing. I had $5 in my pocket. I needed a drink but knew I could not sleep out in the cold. In the town there was an old hotel that had been converted into a boarding house.

I approached the landlady and asked her how much it would cost for a room. She told me $5.

“I’ve only got two dollars”, I told her. If I gave her $5, I would have nothing left for a bottle of plonk.

She reluctantly agreed to give me a room. Delighted, I bought a bottle of plonk, went up to the room and slept. I intended to carry on my journey to the Eastern States next morning. I had only the clothes I stood up in. I took a shower but I could not shave as I did not have a razor. But there was a fellow in the bathroom shaving and I asked him if he would mind if I used his razor as I was on the road and had sent my gear on ahead.

“No worries”, he said. “Bring it down to room 7 when you’ve finished.”

When I got to room 7, he was getting dressed in a police uniform. My immediate reaction was fear. I had better get back on the road and get out of here. I sensed danger.

Ten minutes later, I walked down the stairs and was confronted by the landlady.

She said, “You don’t have any money and you don’t have anywhere to go. How would you like to work for me for a few days? It will help us both.”

It seemed a good idea, but something told me to get out. Instead, I stayed. I worked for three days, chopping wood, weeding the garden and doing various odd jobs. Then, I decided to get back on the road. My luck was running out as the policeman who lived in the boarding house seemed to be sizing me up.

On Saturday afternoon I got on the road, a bottle of wine and some money in my pocket and feeling like a king. I sat on the side of the road until dusk. I wore only a shirt and pants, the bottle of plonk nearly empty. It was getting dark and cold. What could I do?

I decided to hitch-hike back to town to get another bottle of plonk. Before long an old ute stopped and picked me up. The driver, an old Italian named Joe, asked me what I did and when I told him I was a bricklayer, he almost threw his arms around me.

“Do you want a job?” he asked.

Southern Cross, a small town did not carry a bricklayer. This man felt he had struck the jackpot. He took me home. I was relieved when we walked into the kitchen and there on the table was a flagon of wine. We sat down to drink together.

Next morning, Joe showed me over his farm. It was big and he seemed well off. He pointed out four cars. One of them was a white Valiant with push button gear change.

"Would you like to buy it?" he asked.

"Joe", I replied, "I couldn't afford the steering wheel."

"I won it gambling", he said. "It was in settlement for an $800 debt but I don't want it."

The rest of Sunday we boozed. I worried about two things. How was I going to perform on the job next morning without booze and secondly, I knew the coppers were on to me. And here I was, broke, trying to get back to Sydney and this man had offered me the job of building a brick house. Would I take the chance and stay or just do one or two days work, get some money and shoot through? I decided to sort it out in the morning.

Next day we went to the building site. I was delighted. It was all rough brick work, which suited me down to the ground. My worries about drink proved unnecessary as Joe had a flagon of claret in the car.

He said, "Have a couple of charges before you start and whenever you feel like it."

All I had to do was perform. With the plonk, it was not difficult and I soon settled down to a fast pace. Joe was labouring for me. He was about sixty and before long he was asking me to slow down. I wanted to set a hard pace to feel him out and then find the speed he wanted to work. By lunch time I had worn him out. He took me to the pub, bought me a counter lunch and some beer and said, "You are too fast for me. I'll have to get another labourer to help you."

He then made a significant offer. "You stay and finish the house, I'll pay your wages, pay your board in my daughter's boarding house and when you complete the job, I'll give you that Valiant car."

I had to stay. The coppers could lock me up or I would drive to Sydney in a Valiant car with $700 or $800 in my pocket.

We completed the first day without incident. Half full of claret, I worked well. At knock-off time, Joe took me to his daughter's boarding house. The first thing I noticed was a ten gallon keg of claret in the kitchen. After showering, I went into the dining room for dinner. Lo and behold, there were two policemen boarding there! I froze. They seemed to know who I was, and although very polite, they gave me a funny look.

I had started work on the third day and about ten o'clock a car pulled up with the two policemen in it. They got out, putting on their caps. I knew the power of the bastards and I also knew why they were there. They walked straight over to me.

"What's your name?" He opened what I thought to be a magazine, but it was the 'Police Gazette'. He showed me a page containing my photograph and particulars, saying, "You had better come with us. There's a warrant out for you for maintenance."

Not surprised, I replied, "Hang on a minute. I'll see Joe and tell him."

I walked round the back of the job, went to Joe's car and swallowed half a flagon of claret.

Joe asked me how much the warrant was for, as he was willing to pay it, but when I told him it was $1,300, he freaked out.

"If it wasn't so huge", he said, "I would pay it but it's too much."

They put me in the police car and drove me to the Southern Cross Police Station where they took my particulars and locked me up. The lockup was about three hundred yards from the station. It was built of weatherboard on the outside and the inside was lined with bars.

It was mid-summer and I noted that the grass around the building was dry, about three feet high and very thick. My first thought was fire! If that grass caught fire while I was inside, I would get burnt to death. I was terrified.

There were two cells and a small exercise yard all under the same roof. As the cells were not locked, I had access to both cells and the yard. The claret was wearing off and I knew what I was in for. I was going to have to dry out here. The sentence was seventy seven days.

If the grass caught fire, how would I get out? In order to preserve my sanity, I had to keep this out of my mind because added to this fear was the torment of drying out while confined behind bars. I determined to do it one day at a time. I had learned to pray a little, even though with little faith.

Somehow, I got through that first night. The next morning the Sergeant came with my breakfast of slops and told me that he would let me out through the day to work in the garden, but if I attempted to escape, he would make sure I got at least three years! I knew escape was futile. Southern Cross was in the middle of nowhere and to get a ride out of there would have been difficult. I would stay and do my time.

During the night, I had pondered on why I had not been picked up for maintenance by the police during my stay in Albany. It was simple. The Sergeant told me that the warrant had not been issued until after I had left Albany.

At seven o'clock every morning, the Sergeant would let me out. I would work in the yard all day and be locked up at tea time. The fear of fire had become uppermost in my mind, so on my first day at working, I got a hammer and hid it in my cell. At least I would now be able to smash the lock should a fire break out. This eased my mind.

It was not long before the Sergeant and the three constables realized that I was a good worker. I not only dug most of their yard and planted vegetables, but constructed a barbecue for the Sergeant, made a swimming pool for his ducks and did little jobs for his wife.

One day, they said to me, "We wish we hadn't picked you up, but it's too late now."

I had been there about three weeks when the Sergeant, a solid man of twenty two stone, took me into the pantry of his house and said, "Will you clean this up?"

He had made a home brew – eighty six bottles in all – and had stored them in the pantry. He had used too much sugar and the bottles had started blowing. As big as he was, he was frightened to touch them in case they blew up in his hands.

Would I clean it up! Of course I would! He asked me to stack the full bottles in a box in the garage, which I did – probably about twenty or thirty of them. I then cleaned up all the broken glass and, in doing so, put some in a box with some bottle necks with the caps still intact and hid them at the back of the garage. My scheme was that, while the Sergeant was out during the day, I could pinch a bottle of beer from the box and then throw some broken glass and a bottle neck in the box with some water so it would look as though a bottle had exploded, when in fact, it was in my cell. As I worked through the day, I had a bottle of home brew to look forward to when I was locked up at night, and it would help me sleep.

When the Sergeant asked me sometime later if I would like to help him bottle up another eighty six bottles, I was delighted! When we had finished, I asked him if he would like me to stick it in the shed in case it blew up.

He looked down at me with a knowing expression and replied, "No. We'll put it in the pantry."

That was all he said, but I knew that he knew I had been knocking off his booze.

I had been locked up for forty two days and, mentally, it was very trying. There came a night, when, nearly asleep, I heard the door opening. An aboriginal lady was crying and protesting because she was being locked up in the next cell. She continued wailing after the Sergeant left. I put up with it as long as I could and then walked out into the exercise yard and stood at the bars of her cell.

I said, "What the hell's wrong with you?"

She replied, "I want my Harry. They've locked me up for being drunk."

I said, "Fuck your Harry! You'll only be here four hours and then you'll get out."

"How long have you been in here?" she asked.

"Forty two days", I told her. "I murdered my wife and they're going to take me to the maximum security prison at Kalgoorlie tomorrow to sentence me."

She looked at me in terror and I did not hear another sound from her.

The days dragged on and I fought for my sanity every night and prayed and it must have worked. Release day came! I had the $70 Joe had paid me and I hurried to the pub. While in the lockup, the Sergeant had praised me to the locals as a top tradesman and he had arranged a lot of work for me, but I knew his attempts had been in vain because my alcoholism had progressed to the stage where I was totally unreliable. I so much wanted to lead a normal life and do the jobs he had lined up for me but I knew it was impossible.

The Sergeant said to me, "Go back to the Eastern States then, and get lost in the crowd."

I made for Kalgoorlie, intending to work there for a few days and then try to hitch-hike to Sydney. I had to get out of Western Australia or I would be locked up again.

I got a job there, but I ended up in hospital. In a drunken stupor, I dropped a concrete block on my foot, breaking it. Once again, how could I get the alcohol I must have?

One of the labourers I had met on the job visited me, smuggling in a dozen cans of beer which I put in my locker.

The doctor could not set my foot in plaster until the swelling subsided. I wanted to get out, there and then, and would have done so had I not had the booze in my locker. In my wheelchair, I would go to the toilet and drink the precious cans of beer. This made hospital bearable.

The doctor still would not put my foot in plaster and my workmate had arranged a lift to Perth if I could leave that day. I would be able to stay at his place in Perth until my foot mended.

When I asked the doctor to discharge me, he said, "I can't. If you leave you will forfeit your worker's compensation."

"I don't care", I told him. "Bring me the discharge form."

He pleaded with me but I insisted and, signing the form, I left the hospital immediately.

My foot was still swollen and I could hardly walk but my friend Barry had arranged the lift to Perth. We went straight to a pub at Coolgardie where we stayed the night. We left for Perth early next morning with a cargo of booze in the boot. I only remember arriving at Barry's house in Perth.

It was not long before I was back in hospital. Because of the way I was walking on my injured foot, I slipped a disc in my lower back which immobilised me. In Royal Perth Hospital, I was put in traction. This time I really was beaten! There was no way I could get a drink now. There I was, trussed up like a Christmas turkey, in bed, with my legs up in the air and heavy weights hanging from them. How the hell was I going to get out?

Barry came to see me and, as it was New Year's Eve, he bought a bottle of Johnnie Walker. He was putting it in my locker when the Sister caught him. She confiscated it and my heart sank, but I knew that somehow I would get that bottle back.

The next day the same Sister was on duty. There were six other men in the ward and I asked them if they would like a drink of scotch for New Year's Day. Two said they would.

To the others who said they didn't care, I said, "When Sister gives you one, give it to me when she has gone."

I called Sister and said, "Sister, it's New Year's Day. You have a bottle of Scotch of mine. I would like to shout you all a drink."

"A very good idea, Mr Welsh. Very kind of you."

She went out, got glasses and poured a shot of whisky for all the patients, and then left the ward. I drank mine as well as those given to the non-drinkers, who brought their glasses to me.

After five whiskeys, I was half cut and wanted some more. Against the anxious advice of the other patients, I removed the harness from my legs and released the weights. Freed, I dressed and crawled out of the hospital, the pain in my back almost unbearable. I got down to a bar and ran into Clive, a brickie I had worked with in the past. We got drunk and he took me back to his place.

I stayed with him for several weeks. My back was so bad, I had to attend a physiotherapist every day and for several weeks I managed to control my drinking.

One day, Clive said to me, "I'm going to Adelaide, Geordie. Do you want to come?"

He explained why he was going. He was separated from his wife and she had put their two children into a home. He intended to get them out and shoot through to Adelaide. He needed someone to help him. I was only too eager to do so. I knew the torment of being locked up in a home.

He had arranged to visit his children at the home and take them out for the day. In the morning, it was raining heavily. He picked up the children in his old Holden and met me outside the pub round the corner. We filled up with petrol, bought some tucker and a swag of booze and took off.

The trip over the Nullarbor was a bloody nightmare! There we were – two chronic alcoholics abducting two children, six and ten years old and knowing that if we were caught, we would land up in gaol for a long time. This was constantly on our minds. We lost a muffler and the old Holden sounded like a Sherman tank. After five and a half days, we tried to sneak quietly into Adelaide and avoid the police, who we were sure would be on the lookout for us. We went straight to the Central Methodist Mission where Clive left me to organize something for the children.

At the Mission, there was a place called 'the crypt'. It was the basement of the church and it was here that all the Skid Row alkies hung out during the day. There, we were safe from the coppers and could get a shower, a clean shirt and, if not shaking too much, have a shave. We could stay there until five o'clock and then go to either the Matthew Talbot for a feed or sleep out somewhere.

This was my introduction to dereliction, although I was unaware of it at the time. I was thirty four. Here I saw, for the first time, the near-end results of alcoholism. Here were good men, highly intelligent men, a couple of scientists, teachers, men from all walks of life reduced to nothing.

We would gather in the crypt and share whatever we had. It stank of urine, sweat and vomit and I was a part of it. Booze was not allowed in the crypt, but in desperation, we would smuggle it in. I was introduced to methylated spirits for the first time. One Sunday morning, I was in a shocking state of withdrawal. My whole body was shaking, I was sweating and on the verge of an alcoholic seizure. I had no money, but all in there recognized my predicament.

"Jesus, Mate!" one man said. "You're in a bad way. Here, have a charge of metho."

I had never drunk metho and had vowed never to do so, but here I was, faced with the dilemma of either drinking it or going insane.

My mind went back to the days when people said, "Geordie, you'll finish up on metho. You'll finish up in the gutter."

And here I was! Whether I denied it or not, I was on the road to dereliction. I took the charge of metho which had been broken down with water. I was not sure what it would do to me. I choked swallowing it but the results were amazing. After one mouthful, I started to settle down. It was a miracle! By the third charge, I began to feel normal again.

On Sunday, the Minister came to do his best to give us some hope. We had a high regard for men of the cloth and would never swear or be discourteous in their presence. It was against the Skid Row code to show discourtesy to anyone connected with St. Vincent de Paul, women, children and animals.

Every Sunday, we sat in rows waiting for the Minister to arrive. Even though I had thrown God out of the window, I always looked forward to the Minister's arrival. We sang hymns like "The Old Rugged Cross", "There's a Green Hill Far Away", and "Rock of Ages". Hymns like these and the mention of Jesus always brought tears to my eyes and would stir something deep down inside. I would look around and see other men crying too. They were hard, strong men living the life of dereliction and they were crying like little children.

What moved us to such emotion? Was it the kindness or the spirituality? After the hymns, the Minister would read us a few lines from the Bible. I knew what he read was right and my shame and remorse were unbearable.

Sometimes, I went back to A.A., often filthy, dirty and sick. But I was not only learning more about my disease, I was living it too! Then came my first visit to a psychiatric centre. Another step down. I had been admitted to general hospitals for alcoholism but never to an asylum. It was one of the 'yets' – the yet to happen – that they had told me about in A.A.

At a meeting, they said to me, "We will have to put you into hospital, Geordie. To try and dry out on your own would be dangerous."

They took me to Hillcrest Hospital. There, for the first time, I saw people suffering from Korsakoff's Syndrome – the result of many years of heavy drinking. The brain cells are destroyed and a human being is reduced to a vegetable. They were like little children. The saliva ran from their lips, the snot from their noses and incontinent, they would urinate themselves. In the dining room they had to be fed. If left on their own, they would pick up the food with their hands and, in attempting to get it to their mouths, would spread it across their faces.

It appalled me. To think that these people had once been

respected members of society! I was not ready to admit that I was travelling down the same road.

I stayed in the hospital for three days before shooting through. I could put up with the sight of sorrowful victims of alcohol but I had been affected by my years in institutions and I could not bear being locked up.

I bummed around Adelaide, doing what I could to earn a quid. I mixed with the boys. We drank metho, plonk, anything we could get hold of. We swallowed pills too – valium, librium, largactil, anything to alleviate the suffering. Often we drank 'heavy' – metho mixed with plonk.

Here, I learned the Skid Row code. Like any other society, Skid Row has rules that one has to learn and obey. You don't steal from one another. You can steal from anyone else, but not from a 'stiff' (a derelict). If you have money, you share it. Should another man be suffering and you have a drink, you share it whether you know him or not or even if you dislike him. The same with your tobacco and cigarette bumpers. Should you break the code, you are 'cuffed'. This means you are Out. If you are made Out in Skid Row, you have had it, because you need each other to survive. We shared our dole cheques and our sickness benefits and survived as best we could.

I was getting locked up regularly. The police in Adelaide gave us a hard time. I would be walking down the street when a police car would pull up. They would ask my name, where I was going, where I worked and did I have any warrants. I was scared of powder blue cars and scared of being locked up. Through all my drinking, I dreaded this more than anything. There were times when I got locked up twice in the same day! I would be released in the morning, meet one of the boys who had a bottle of plonk and we would find an alleyway where we could drink it. After blacking out, I would come to in the same cell I had been thrown out of that morning!

The Adelaide lockup was the only one I had been in where you were locked up 'one out' or by yourself. It was bad, because there was no-one to talk to. It was dark, it stank, the bed was a block of wood and the pillow a big wooden wedge. And this was 1972, not 1772. One suffered in there alone with a dirty toilet in the corner.

When one is coming off the booze, especially metho and plonk, the pain of dehydration is indescribable. The police could never bring me enough water to quench my thirst so I drank the water from the toilet. The trick was to flush it and, as the water was pouring down the back you held a mug to catch it as this was the cleanest part. I would swallow the water, hold it down for a moment or two and then throw it up. I would have to do this all the time I was in the cell, no matter how long I was there. It was both mental and physical agony.

I started to pray to God. "God, get me out of this and I promise I won't do it again. I promise I'll go back to A.A. and stay sober." But they were promises I could not keep.

About this time, the Methodist Mission sent me up to their rehabilitation farm in the Adelaide Hills. It was called Kuipto Colony. It was a beautiful, serene place. The food was excellent. There were counsellors and a Minister to help us. We occupied ourselves in the vegetable and flower gardens and did work needed to maintain the buildings. They soon discovered I could mould and they gave me a small shed to set up as a workshop. This gave me a sense of responsibility and lifted my self-esteem. I built two benches, designed flower pots and bird baths, making and cutting moulds and showed other alkies how to use them. The training given to me by Pio at Bindoon was very valuable.

I made enough progress to be transferred to Shaftesbury House in Adelaide – a halfway house that was part of the Kuipto Colony rehabilitation structure. Things went alright for a while, but one of my biggest enemies was loneliness. To remain sober, I had to stay away from my old acquaintances, but loneliness and the nostalgia for Skid Row soon took me back to the bottle and the merry-go-round.

It was as bad as before. One freezing, wet, windy night, another alkie and I had half a bottle of plonk between us. The only shelter we could find was a disused toilet. We took turns to sit on the toilet seat. When the floor became too cold, we changed places. To make matters worse there was a large gap under the door which allowed the rain and wind in to further add to our discomfort. We could not get warm and eventually we sat together on the floor and cuddled each other to try to keep out the cold.

It was not that there was homosexuality amongst Skid Row

alcoholics but it was not unusual to cuddle each other for warmth and comfort.

There were many ways to keep warm. One method was to slide old newspaper up the back and front of the shirt.

An alkie said to me one day, "Geordie, which newspaper do you use for a blanket?"

"The morning paper", I replied.

"I use the evening paper", he said. "It seems to have more warmth."

My ulcer perforated again and as I had lost half my blood, I had to be operated on. In the operation, a partial gastrostomy, half of my stomach was removed. Before I had recovered, I developed pneumonia and was close to death. In three weeks, I had had three operations as well as pneumonia.

They started to feed me crushed ice every forty minutes to get my stomach working again. I had been fed on a drip which was alternated between my wrists which became painfully swollen. The first dose of ice made me thirsty. Just prior to it, the nurse had rubbed my back with methylated spirits. To add to this, the doctor was reducing my intake of drugs. With these three factors – the thirst, the smell of metho and the withdrawal from heavy drugs – I was set up to drink.

I tore the drip out of my arm and got out of bed. I had not been on my feet for seven weeks and my legs could hardly hold my weight.

The patient in the next bed moved to press the buzzer to call the Sister. "You're mad" he cried. "Where are you going?"

I picked up a water jug and said, aggressively, "If you press that buzzer, I'll hit you over the head with this."

I saw the alarm in his eyes as he put the buzzer down.

I managed to pull my dressing gown on. I was on the third floor. I struggled down the stairs with one arm around my stomach and the other gripping the rails. I rested in the hospital canteen, intending to walk out to a hotel a few yards down the road.

What insanity! Here I was hardly able to walk, weak, barefooted, thirty two stitches in my abdomen, dressed only in pyjamas and a hospital dressing gown and making my way to a hotel! Such is the power of alcohol!

God must have given me a moment of sanity. I realized I

could not make it to the hotel so I ordered a milkshake and a packet of cigarettes. It was not long before Sister arrived in a state of panic.

"We've found you! Come on, back to the ward." She couldn't believe what she saw. I was smoking and drinking a milkshake. "Both of those things can kill you." She took me back to the ward where she put me back to bed.

"Come on, Mr Welsh. We've got to put this drip back in your wrist."

"You're not!" I said.

She thought I was joking and moved to put the drip into place.

"No!" I cried, defiantly.

She realized now that I was serious and called the doctor.

In a condescending voice, he said, "Come on, Mr Welsh. Hold out your arm and we'll put the drip back in."

I had made up my mind and again refused. "You are not going to put that drip in my arm."

"Please don't be foolish", the doctor said. "You can't eat and this is the only way we can feed you. If we don't put it back, you'll die."

I still refused. He turned to the Sister and asked her to get a form. In her absence, he pleaded with me but I still said no. Sister returned with the form. He made one last plea.

"Alright, Mr Welsh. Sign this form which will exonerate me and the hospital staff from any blame, not if you die but when you die."

I signed it.

He then let me have it. "On three occasions we have battled to save your life and here you are, after all our work, going to throw it away.

He abused me in front of all the ward. I said to him, "I'm not going to die."

He shook his head and walked away.

I knew, despite my condition, that I would live. I stayed in the hospital for three more weeks, most of the time with a drain tube in my back. When the wounds in my stomach healed, I knew the time had come to leave.

One of the specialists said, "We don't want to let you out

yet. You are not strong enough."

But I meant to get out whether they liked it or not, no matter what my condition.

"If you don't let me go, I'll leave."

I meant it and he relented. He agreed to discharge me on the following Monday.

Another specialist had a final word to me on Monday. "You know that you are a chronic alcoholic. We have done a lot of work on you. We've saved your life. Please, please Mr Welsh, don't drink! If you do, it will kill you. I have no more to say. Good luck!"

I was supposed to go to a clinic every day and have the wound in my back dressed, but I only attended occasionally and then always drunk.

Sister would shake her head and say, "You know you are supposed to come here every day. If this thing turns infectious, you will die."

I bummed around Port Adelaide, but the coppers were getting too heavy for me. I knew there were three warrants out for my arrest and I did not want to be locked up, so I left Adelaide.

I will never know how I got to Shepparton in Victoria! I was broke, sick and needed a drink. I had a beautiful pair of dress boots which I had probably stolen. I sold them in a secondhand shop for $4, exchanging them for a pair of thongs. I now had enough to get drunk.

At one stage, I went back to A.A. Some bastard had the audacity to say, "Jesus loves you."

"What crap", I thought. "Look at the things He's done to me and you say He is kind and loving! You have to be joking!"

From Shepparton, I found my way to Pentridge Gaol. I had been on the metho for some time and was eating very little. One freezing night, I came out of a blackout. I had half a bottle of plonk and nowhere to sleep. I stumbled into the scrub and got under a tree. It was so cold, I broke some branches from a tree and put them over me to keep warm. I slept on top of my booze so that I would not lose it. I dozed off and went into the rats. When I woke, it was dark and I could not find my plonk. I panicked. I had to get a drink.

I remembered a place where I had boarded in brief moments

of sobriety. It was owned by an Italian and he had a lot of home-made wine in a cupboard in the outside laundry. I headed there. The consequences did not concern me. I had to have a drink at any cost. I grabbed two bottles of grappa and ran. It was about six o'clock in the morning.

I sat on the footpath, drinking the grappa, a strong heavy wine which had almost the same effect as metho. A powder blue car pulled up and a plain clothes detective got out. I did not care. I was beyond caring.

"Where did you get that wine?" he asked.

"I stole it", I told him.

He took me to the lockup, telling me I would have to face the 'Beak'. I was terrified of being locked up and knew it would not be long before I went into the DTs and be unable to get a drink to stop them. I was also prone to alcoholic seizures now. These are similar to epileptic fits only worse and without medical attention, can be fatal. There are two types – the grand mal and the petit mal. One usually dies during the third grand mal seizure and I knew I had reached this dangerous stage. I could die in that police cell.

I struggled with the police when they tried to lock me up. They twisted both arms up behind my back so that my thumbs touched the back of my head and it felt as though my arms were being pulled out of their sockets. The pain was excruciating.

Two aboriginal boys were brought into the cell. They too, had been locked up for drunkenness. By now, I was half in the DTs, the pain in my shoulders agonising and I wanted to die. Fortunately, these two boys realized there was something wrong with me and called the Sergeant.

"This man needs a doctor", they told him. "He's sick."

In my semi-demented mind, I heard the Sergeant say, "The doctor says all we can do is give him a drink."

He poured out a pannikin full of wine or something and one of the boys held it to my lips. I was shaking so much I could not hold it myself. I swallowed it in a couple of gulps. It calmed me down. The Sergeant gave me another one which I sipped through the night to make it last.

Next morning, shaking and half-demented, I fronted up to the magistrate. I pleaded guilty and was sentenced to one month in Pentridge to dry out.

I was very frightened. I had not been in a big prison before. I did not fear the prison itself or the inmates, but I was scared of being locked up without a drink.

They put me in the back of a wagon, handcuffed to an aboriginal man – a good chap – and we were carted off to Pentridge.

CHAPTER

5

Ah, Love! Could thou and I, with Fate conspire
To grasp this sorry Scheme of Things entire.
Would not we shatter it to bits – and then
Re-mould it nearer to the Heart's Desire.
Omar Khayyam

At Pentridge, I submitted to the procedure of being locked up in a maximum security prison. To survive, I kept my eyes and ears open and my mouth closed. During the day, I worked in the laundry and at night, until lights out, I read books from the library.

Pentridge Gaol was another step down the ladder of degradation. I had learnt in A.A. that if I continued to drink, life would get worse. It was all happening to me, but I denied it. It was just that I was having a rough trot.

When I was released, I bummed around Melbourne until sobering up enough to get a job as a kitchen hand in an Indian restaurant in Little Bourke Street. The manager, Gordon, was an understanding man and the staff were pleasant to work with.

But after a week, I got on the booze and Gordon said, "Put yourself in hospital, Geordie, dry out and then come back. Your job will still be here."

I dried out and went back. When this had happened three times, Gordon said, "You're unreal, Geordie. You're a good worker, clean and doing the work of two men. We'd like to train you as second chef."

Here was a golden opportunity! But once again I took to the booze.

After drying out again, I returned, guilty and ashamed. I had abused the kindness and trust of this good man.

I said to him, "Please Gordon, get somebody else. You've given me a fair go, but I can't stay sober and I'll only let you down again."

"That's a shame, Geordie", he said. "You're better than anyone we've ever had." He gave me an extra week's pay, a good reference and then added, "If you ever get sober, come back here and while I'm manager, there'll always be a job for you."

I went to Gordon House, a place for alkies. I worked in the kitchen and tried to stay sober but life was getting heavy. I was on first name terms with the coppers.

Once, while being locked up, I forgot to put my matches and tobacco in the crutch of my undies. It was here we concealed them, as the coppers were not allowed to touch that part of the body when conducting a body search. To be locked up without a smoke and withdrawing, is very cruel. So I put my tobacco under one armpit, matches under the other and held my arms straight down my sides.

The copper smiled. "Raise your right arm, Geordie." As the tobacco fell to the floor, he said, "Now the other one." When the matches hit the floor, he said, still smiling, "Now bend over."

From the bending position, I looked round at him and said, "Do you want my chewing gum, too?"

It was getting too hot, so with a friend, Walter, I decided to go to Brisbane and start a new life. For a while, I got off the booze, found a job, went to A.A. and started to go to church.

I always felt good when I went to a service – never a Catholic one of course. I often cried when singing a hymn. But I could not overcome my background. God was the man with a big stick and a big book. The Catholics had taught me that to get to Jesus I had to go through Mary and the Saints. Other denominations never spoke of them. If God was loving and kind, why were all these nasty things happening to me? He was punishing me. But why?

The sober life didn't last, of course. One day, sick and with no money, I had nowhere to go except St. Vincent de Paul or the Salvation Army flop house. I did not want to go to either and knowing I needed medical help, I took someone's advice and went to the Brisbane Hospital. General hospitals do not normally cater for alkies and alcoholism, but when I got there, a doctor took one look at me, gave me an injection of valium to prevent a seizure and told a nurse to take me up to Ward C. I was shaking badly, my legs so weak I could hardly walk. The nurse was kind and understanding and I, a piece of human wreckage, felt so ashamed.

A sister met us as we got out of the lift and walked into a little room. As we entered, the door closed behind us. The sister pressed the bell of a second door which had a small window in it. Another sister behind the second door opened it and let us in. In all the hospitals I had been in, the entry procedure had never been like this. It was maximum security.

It was a ward for the mentally sick – not just for alcoholics. Down one side were three or four padded cells.

"Oh, my God!" I thought. "I might never get out of here!"

The sister immediately gave me two injections. It was the only hospital I had ever been in where the sister could administer injections without prior instructions from a doctor. I discovered that I was the only alcoholic in there, and I could not communicate with anyone. To retain my sanity, I had to do a lot of praying.

It was in this ward that I saw a screaming man carried in on a stretcher, locked and strapped in a wire cage, totally demented. A seaman, he had drunk the alcohol out of the ship's compass. I thought, surely this man will die or remain insane, but after three days, the staff, in their kindness, brought him out of it. I saw this, another piece of evidence confirming what I had been taught and what I, myself, was facing if I continued drinking. All the time I was terrified of everything and everybody and although the members of A.A. understood me, it was only on Skid Row that I felt at home.

One day, an orderly came in. He looked just like Charlie 'Honk' from Bindoon, a man I still recalled with hate. It is on the third day of withdrawal that one becomes ravishingly hungry and I was suffering badly. The orderly started to make some toast for himself in the kitchen. I asked him if I could have a piece.

He turned and said, "Get out of here, you drunken bum!"

Bindoon and Charlie Honk flashed before me. I saw red.

I picked up a chair to hit him with. Fortunately, the Sister spotted me. She rushed up and, with a lot of authority in her voice, said, "Put that chair down!"

She asked me what had happened and when I told her, she turned to the orderly and said, "You apologise to this man, or I'll report you. You've got no right to speak to patients like that!"

After he had grudgingly apologised, Sister turned to me and said, "You get straight into bed. I'll be there in a minute." She came back and gave me a massive shot of valium and in a few minutes I fell asleep.

I was released from hospital just before the floods of 1973. It rained heavily for a week, reminding me of the tropical storm in Darwin. Once again, I decided to move on and start a new life! I left Brisbane in a blackout and when I came to, I found myself in the middle of a highway. I had no idea where I was, but this was nothing new to me. On previous occasions I had finished up on highways in total darkness, freezing cold and no idea in which direction I was going or how I had got there.

Somebody gave me a lift to a town called Ballina. I couldn't get any farther because the roads were flooded. I stayed there for three days. I had no money but I knew how to survive. I bludged off the Salvation Army, cold bit people in the streets, but knew I would not be able to stay long before the coppers woke up to me.

With a bottle of metho and photos of my children in my bag, I got out. I carried these photos wherever I went. I also carried a book of Michelangelo's work which I had pinched from a library. Sometimes I would sit somewhere, perhaps on a river bank with a bottle of plonk and look through it and cry because of the beauty of his work. With my fingers, I would fondle the paintings and sculptures.

I hit the road and landed in Newcastle, where it did not take me long to hone in on Skid Row. It is always the same with alkies. When we hit a new town, we automatically find the boys. Some of them I had met before. This is not unusual. In any city or town, you always bump into somebody you've met somewhere else. A couple I knew showed me the ropes. I learnt where I could get a quid, which priests and ministers I could bite, where all the snookers were, the areas the coppers patrolled in a minesweeper (pickup wagon), where the Matthew Talbot was, the Sallies, Lifeline – all the essential information a good alkie on Skid Row needs to know.

On my 38th birthday, I was admitted to a psychiatric centre in Newcastle called Watt Street. The admitting sister looked at me, sweating and shaking.

Filling in a form, she looked up and said, "You'd be about fifty five, wouldn't you?"

She had not said it facetiously. It was an honest assessment. When I told her my true age, she could not hide her surprise.

During my stay there, I resolved to go back to A.A. Lying in bed, I took serious stock of my life for probably the first time. I knew I was a top tradesman and capable of working hard. I knew what was happening to me and had been taught what the results would be if I did not change my lifestyle. I made up my mind that I would try. I had seen other examples in A.A., many as bad as I was and who were now living decent lives. There may be a chance for me.

I came out of hospital well and fit. At that stage, it did not take me long to recover physically. I could use a trowel and work hard and I thought that that was what the A.A. members meant by 'being well'. It was a mistake.

It was at a meeting that I met Cathy. She was gorgeous. Also an alkie, she came from Scotland and was known as Scotch Cathy. We fell in love. Working and staying sober, I had bought an old Holden for $95, was going to A.A. and getting some nice clothes together. I had been sober for five months. I had not been sober this long for twenty years. Perhaps I could lead a normal life at last, like the others in A.A. They were happy but they warned me not to get emotionally involved until I had been sober for at least two years.

But I would not listen! I had never had anyone to love and at last I had Cathy and I was not going to let her go, not at any price! I would have died for her.

However, they were right again. They were always right. Cathy and I fought, and it was I who caused the fights.

One day, after a bitter argument, she said, "Geordie, I love you. I would die for you."

It was too much. I couldn't handle the powerful emotion of love; it was new to me. I was obsessed by Cathy. I started to drink.

She took me to Morrisett Hospital, thirty miles away. They nursed me back so that I was able to return to Cathy. I stayed sober for two months. Cathy stayed with me for nine months. I only saw Cathy cry twice.

On one occasion, I was in her lounge. I had the world at my feet. I had Cathy who loved me; she had two beautiful children; she had a home and we were both good workers. But I could not get off the grog. On this occasion, when Cathy was in the bedroom and I was in the lounge with her little girl, I picked up a bottle I had planted under the house. Once I started to drink, I could not stop. Cathy called me into the bedroom. She was crying. Cathy was a strong woman – she had been brought up in Glasgow, but she was gentle too. To see her crying moved me.

She said, "Geordie, I love you. I don't want to see you back on Skid Row. I don't want you to die. I love you. Please don't drink."

Oh, how I wished I could do as she asked! But I knew I had to go on drinking and there was nothing I could do to stop myself. I went back to the lounge and picked up the bottle. The little girl was standing next to me. The tears ran down my face, because I knew I was going to leave.

The little girl, Margo, looked up at me and said, "Geordie, why are you crying?"

She was nine years old. How could I explain to this little girl?

In desperation, Cathy took me back to Morrisett Hospital. As she left, she pleaded with me again.

"We could have a good life together, Geordie. Please, please stop drinking. I will come and see you every day and pray for both of us."

I stayed four hours and then shot through and headed for Cathy's. Half demented, in the DTs and ripe for a seizure, I started to walk. It was thirty miles away.

I kept saying to myself, "Welshie, just keep putting one foot in front of the other. Don't think. Just keep walking."

I arrived at six o'clock in the morning, exhausted. Cathy put me to bed but she had to go to work. She told me to stay in bed and pleaded with me not to drink anything. She promised to come home and look after me.

I needed something to settle me down. I was going mad. I searched the house and found some valium tablets but could not find any methylated spirits. But I did find a bottle of Cathy's perfume called 'Serenity'. I mixed some with water and had a charge of that with the valium. Then I found a few bob in the house and went over to the store and bought a bottle of metho.

By the time Cathy came home, I was out to it. Cathy told me later that when she saw me flat out on the bed, she thought I was dead.

It was no good. I had to leave. I knew I was going back to Skid Row. I took my car. Leaving hurt both of us.

"Geordie, You're going to die" she said.

I did not have the car long. I sold it for $5 in a bar. I needed a flagon of plonk. A couple of nights later, I tried to pinch it from outside the pub. I realized I had sold it too cheaply. I got in, three parts full. As I was about to start it, the door was pulled open.

"You bastard, Geordie! Where do you think you're going?"

Two men dragged me out, threw me to the ground and started kicking me. It was a vicious attack and I lost the use of my left arm for several months.

I had been in Watt Street and Morrisett so many times. I was taken to them by members of A.A., sometimes unconscious, occasionally bashed up. Sometimes the police took me in and sometimes I crawled in. Often, they did not want to admit me. The doctor would take one look at my file, which was becoming as thick as a telephone directory, and say, "No, we've dried you out before. You're only using us up. We're not going to admit you."

The charge nurse would plead with the doctor and if the doctor remained adamant, would go over the doctor's head.

I was always escaping from those places. As soon as I came round, I would start thinking about getting out. On one occasion, I heard someone say that they had a pair of slacks in the spin dryer.

I went down to the laundry and grabbed them. I was wearing my pyjama coat with 'Newcastle Psychiatric Centre' stamped on the back. The pants were too big for me so I put my hands in the pockets to hold them up. I walked out and bumped into a bloke called Pat Murphy. He had a bottle of metho and a bottle of lemonade. I had just pinched two bottles of vodka from a bottle shop. We found an old tin and three quarter filled it with vodka and topped it up with metho and lemonade. We drank this mixture all day and when I was carted back to the hospital, I was horribly sick. At this stage, alcohol no longer made me drunk. It made me stupid and sick – far more sick than drunk. Next day, Pat arrived!

We had no medication and in those circumstances, withdrawal is very cruel. The body and mind scream out for alcohol which is the only thing which will give relief. Pat and I could not bear it, so we rolled up our pyjama pants and shot out the back into a side street. As sick as dogs, shaking like leaves, with sweat pouring from us and with pyjamas stamped N.P.C. we struggled down the street to a pub. It was not long before we were taken back to the ward.

Another time, when I had a few bob, I escaped to the Grand Hotel straight across from the hospital. I had rolled my pyjamas up to the knees. I was withdrawing terribly and was terrified that the publican would recognize the outfit and refuse to give me a bottle. I walked into the bar dressed like that – in a pair of pyjamas with a big stamp on the back and shaking like hell.

The barman took one look and said, "Hey! You're from across the road, aren't you?"

I said, "No, I've just come up from the beach."

He looked at me and was about to give me a bottle when a voice from the end of the bar called out, "Hello, Lionel. How are you?"

It was one of the nurses from Watt Street. He walked up to me and taking me by the arm, said, "Come on. I'm taking you back."

Once, at Watt Street, I took a massive seizure. I was sitting in the dining room hanging on to the table struggling to keep my sanity. The table and everything on it was shaking. I woke up in bed.

A counsellor came in and said, "Geordie, you can only take three seizures like that. They're called grand mals. You are also close to becoming a wet brain. If you drink again, you'll either have a grand mal or wet brain. Either way, you'll die."

Watt Street was an Admission Centre and we were locked up with all types of patients. One day, I was trying to eat my dinner in the dining room but getting the food to my mouth was almost impossible. It took every ounce of physical effort to raise the spoon because of my shaking body. The girl opposite, a beautiful, refined looking girl with lovely long hair, picked up her bowl of boiling hot soup and tipped it over her head and did not bat an eyelid!

On another occasion, a patient walked around the dining room and at random, picked up cups and saucers and plates from the tables and smashed them against the walls.

I do not blame these people. They were sick. Society had put them there.

In Watt Street, therapy sessions were held every morning. All the alkies would be in a room with two psychiatrists. I am sure one of them was mad himself! They both gave us a hard time. They put us in what they called the hot seat, sitting between the two of them. It would be the first day off the booze, with terrible withdrawals and they would start throwing questions, awful questions, one after the other, like a machine gun. My head was so bad, I could hardly take it.

They would say, "Do you know where you are? You are in a unit for recycling piss-pots. This is society's garbage heap. This place is here for when society has finished with you. You are nothing but social garbage. You are nobody any more! You have no place in society."

It drove me so mad that one day, I got up and, as sick as I was, I grabbed one of them by the throat.

My alcoholism had progressed rapidly and I would collapse into a bad state of the DTs and take seizures. I would hear voices all the time. I would flush the toilet and hear a brass band! I would turn on a tap and the Philharmonic Orchestra would play! I would open a fridge door and Louis Armstrong would sing! At night, people were going to kill me and horrible things would come out of the wall. I would see things I cannot describe and all the artistic talents of the world could not draw or paint the things I saw in the DTs. They were terrifying.

One day I was passing a little church and some people were standing outside. I thought these Christians would be good for a bob or two. Before I realized what was happening, I found myself inside. I was shaking the chair to pieces, the sweat pouring out of me and all I wanted to do was get out.

The man who had brought me in said, "Stay with us. You'll be alright. God will look after you."

I wondered how I could get out without offending him. But I had to get out to get a drink.

I asked him, "Where's the toilet?"

"Come with me, Brother", he said, "and I'll show you."

Usually the toilets at church are outside but he pointed to a door at the end of a passage. I panicked. How would I get out? Perhaps there would be a window. There was no window, but there was a big cupboard. Out of curiosity, I opened it, hoping to find, perhaps, a bottle of something. But in front of me was a big bottle of methylated spirits, two thirds full. I could not believe it. I said, "Thank you, God."

With shaking hands, I held the bottle under the water tap, shook it and took a charge. I gave myself two more good belts and put it back before making my way back to the hall. I started to settle down. Metho is good like that. I did not mind being there so much and started listening to the Minister. What he said made sense and I wished I could be like these people. They were happy and secure. I had no hope of anything. I had given up. The chances of ever getting sober or ever doing anything with my life were gone.

I said to the guy next to me, "I'll have to go to the toilet again. I've got diarrhoea."

He said, "That's O.K. Brother."

So I would go to the toilet and have a belt of metho and come back feeling good. Nearing the end of the service, I had settled down peacefully. The Minister could have spoken all day and night and I could not have cared less. There was still half a bottle of metho in the cupboard! Just before the service finished, I went to the toilet and stuffed the bottle into my jacket pocket.

On my way out, the guy said, "By Gee! You're a different

man to the person who came in with me. God has sure done something for you. He's worked a miracle."

I had been going to A.A. off and on for seven years. I had always been treated kindly and with understanding, but by now the members were beginning to take the gloves off.

"Geordie", they said, "it's time you got fair dinkum. You're just mucking around. Don't come within a hundred miles of my place, Geordie. I'll call the police if you do! If you ring me, I'll put the phone down. If you want to talk to me do it at A.A. meetings."

One day, I stood at the reception desk at the lockup. The constable, his feet up on the desk, was rooting around in my bag, the bag which contained the letters and photos of my kids. I would not let go of it. The things in it were the last shred of decency I had – the memory of my children. And here was this man, lounging in his chair, mocking a letter from my little girl, reading it aloud to all and sundry in a scornful way.

I cannot describe what happened to me. My heart and soul were torn out. I screamed insanely. Here was the last decent thing I had and this bastard was desecrating it. I went crazy.

I screamed like a maniac, "I'll kill you, you bastard."

I tried to jump over the counter to kill him. It took three policemen to get me to a padded cell. It was black and padded all round with big black buttons and with a tiny light in the ceiling and a small round hole in the door. Everything was black. It was about eight feet by eight feet. I knew I had to calm myself and that if I pondered on where I was and what had happened, I would go crazy, so I sat against a wall, put my head in my hands and prayed.

At intervals, I got up and walked over to the door, cupped my hands around the small hole, put my mouth to my hands and at the top of my voice, I screamed abuse at the policemen. Then I sat down and prayed again.

At some stage, they transferred me to an ordinary cell. I stood at the door with my hands wrapped around the bars, looking down the passage, full of hate. It was a terrible hate of society, of God, of these coppers, of everybody. Bindoon came back to me and I can't describe my feelings at that moment. The hate festered inside me like a boil. I was like a wild animal.

Alcohol had reduced me to this.

Here I was, locked up in one of society's prisons for no other reason than that I drank. I stood there at the bars, my hands wrapped around them.

A young copper came up and said, "Let go of the bars." (When you are locked up, you are not allowed near the door.)

"He repeated, "Let go of the bars."

I looked at him with a terrible hate. I swore at him, using vile language. I hated him for what they had done to my daughter's letter. I screamed profanities at him.

He insisted, "I'll make you let go."

I thought, "We'll see." The determination of Bindoon came back to me. There was no way I was going to let go of those bars. I didn't care what he did.

He took out his baton and held it up. "Are you going to let go?"

"You can smash my knuckles to pulp, but I'm not going to let go!"

With that, he gave a whack across the knuckles with the baton. I was so insane, I did not even feel it. I looked back at him with contempt and hate and continued to abuse him.

"Are you going to let go?"

"No way!"

He smashed me across one set of knuckles and then the other.

I turned and said, "You can bash my hands right into these bars, but I won't let go. You cannot hurt me with that thing any more than I've been hurt already. You can bash me to death if you like."

He put the baton away and looked at me. I raised my finger to my head and pointed to my brain, saying, "I mean in here. That thing you've got can't hurt me."

It was not the last time I found myself in that padded cell. On one occasion, I played up so much they asked me if there was someone they could contact to get me out. I gave them the name of a member of A.A. and he came and got me out.

They said to him, "Get that wild animal out of here! The bastard's mad."

Back in Morriset Hospital, I took a drinking glass to the toilet, intending to commit suicide. I felt no fear, just empty inside. I sat on the toilet with the glass poised to drive it up my arm. I knew how to do it.

But a voice said, "When you were a little boy, they taught you that if you take your own life you'll go to hell and hell is forever. If there is a hell, even a million to one chance and its only as half as bad as what you are going through now, do you want to go there? It is for ever."

I put the glass on the floor and walked back to the ward.

I would lie on my bed and talk to God. "Please let me die. Please!" In my insanity, I would sometimes see a beautiful hand just above my head. "Reach up", a voice would say, "and take hold of my hand. Don't let go. Last time you let go and this is what happened. You're back here again. If you let go, next time will be worse."

I was picked up on a vagrancy charge. I was nearly forty two years of age, could hardly walk and the detective had to help me into the court room. I was terrified and knew I was on the verge of the DTs or a seizure. When the Judge addressed me, I tried to stand up but my legs would not hold me. The Judge gave me permission to sit.

I was given one month on a vagrancy charge. He looked at me and asked, "How old are you?"

When I mumbled, "Forty one," he glanced around the court room, shaking his head. I knew what he was thinking. I must have looked seventy.

Except for my love for Cathy, I was now devoid of any feeling. My friends in Skid Row were dying around me like flies. Some of them suffered horrible deaths and three of them were murdered. One of them, Norman, was kicked to death in an empty house. Two others were found by the railway line, both murdered. I had drunk with these men many times. I had slept out with them and in the same places where they had met their deaths!

Once, I was taken to Maitland Gaol on the back of a big paddy wagon and was handcuffed to a man who was getting thirteen years for rape! I was terrified. But he and his mate were happy. You would have thought they were going to a holiday camp! I had only got a month and this bloke had got thirteen years, but to me, in my condition, a month was worse than a lifetime. My only crime was that I had picked up a drink. I had not murdered or raped anyone. I had been picked up on the beach, on my own, with a bottle of plonk.

I would urinate and excrete myself; vomit over myself and spew up bile. And the members of A.A. had told me that all these things would happen – every single one of them!

I gave up. I did not want to go on.

But God did hear my prayers! I landed at Dr Chandler's surgery, a wreck, in a condition only a doctor could describe, an emaciated piece of human – completely beaten. I staggered into his surgery, not drunk, just sick and hoping I could get a dollar from him to buy a bottle of metho.

There were a lot of people sitting in the waiting room, but Dr Chandler took one look at me and led me into his consulting room. He looked at me and shook his head. He told one of the nurses to give me a cup of coffee.

He said, "Geordie, I'll have to put you into hospital."

"You can't," I said miserably. "I'm barred from Morriset and Woodlands. They won't have a bar of me."

He looked at me sympathetically and said, "You are going to die, Geordie. We have to get you into hospital."

I remember saying to him, "I don't care! I wish I could die! I can't take this anymore. I can't go on. I can't get sober. I just want to die!"

"I'm a doctor. I can't let you die, Geordie. I must get you into hospital."

"You can't," I said. "I'm barred. Just give me 50 cents so I can get a bottle of metho and straighten myself out."

"You know I can't do that." He went out, but left a nurse with me. When he came back, he said, "I'm getting you up to Morriset."

"You can't get me into Morriset," I said. "I've been there so many times, they've classed me as a no-hoper."

He smiled. "I told them they must take you for six weeks voluntarily or they have you for twelve months under the Inebriates Act. They've agreed to take you for six weeks."

He sat down as the nurse left the room. "I've gone to a lot of trouble to get you in there, Geordie. If you leave before six weeks, don't ever come near my surgery again. I'm sick of you."

I loved that man. He was the instrument that God used to

save my life. He rang for a taxi and while helping me in, said to the driver, "Whatever you do, don't let this man out. Take him to Ward 18 at Morriset Hospital. Don't stop. Don't let him out. If he vomits, excretes or urinates in your car, I'll pay for it. Just get him up there, or he'll die."

Sitting in the taxi, all I wanted was a drink. I was already scheming how to get out of the cab. Dr Chandler paid the driver for the thirty two mile journey from his own pocket.

Once the taxi started, I lost the urge to escape. I knew I was too sick and, anyway, if I did get out, I would be picked up by the coppers and die in a gaol.

I don't remember arriving at Morriset, but I do remember some days later, walking around the ward thinking, "How long will I stay sober this time? If I can stay sober one day more than last time – just one more day – I will be making progress. I thought of all the things I had been taught by A.A. and how I had ignored them.

Then, quietly, it came to me that I could walk out of that hospital and never drink again. One day at a time, I need never drink again. I knew then, it was over! The members of A.A. had been saying for eight years, "Geordie, you keep trying and coming to us and you'll know when you've got IT".

At that moment, I knew that my drinking was over. I just knew it! Thank God! Thank God I kept going to A.A. for eight years! Thank God it's finished. It's over! I cried inwardly. The suffering was over. It was a miracle. I acknowledged to myself that I had had nothing to do with this. It had nothing to do with my own strength or determination. I had not made up my mind that I was not ever going to drink again – none of these things. It was a MIRACLE.

I went to Sister Dolly, the charge nurse. On many previous visits, she had begged and cajoled me to stop drinking.

I said to her, "You know Dolly, I won't ever have to come here again."

She looked at me in a strange way and said, "Geordie, I don't think you'll have to either."

I thought a lot about it. I realized that members of A.A. had got me out of gaols, taken me to hospitals, prayed over me, shed tears for me and had never really told me what to do! They had been trying to stop my suffering – that was all. They had been watching a good man slowly destroying himself. I realized too, that there was a God, a real God and that people do not perform miracles. This was a miracle.

So many times I had felt alone; that I was left hanging in the sky like a bird frightened to fly or in the middle of an ocean, a fish terrified of the water.

In spite of the promise I had made to Dr Chandler, I discharged myself. I knew that hospitals could only make me physically well. They could not cure the mental and spiritual aspect of my disease.

With the help of A.A., I could do it. One day at a time, I could handle anything. I had seen other people in A.A. who had been through experiences worse than mine and they were living decent, clean lives with the help of others in Alcoholics Anonymous. I knew I could do it too.

The drink had been removed from my life. The dilemma of change that confronted me did not have to be handled alone. Although the task was difficult, I need not be frightened. God had taken the booze from me. This I had learned in A.A. I no longer needed the hospital. A.A. had the tools for me to work with; the rest was up to me.

CHAPTER

6

Who! hath not ate his bread in sorrow
Who! hath not spent the midnight hour
Weeping and waiting for the morrow,
He knows Ye not, Ye heavenly power.

Goethe

I went to Dr Chandler's surgery, fearful of being thrown out because I had not kept my promise. He did not believe me when I told him of my experience. He was not happy about me leaving Morriset.

I asked him, "What is the state of my liver?"

He looked at me and said, "Probably finished the way you've treated it over the years. We'll get a blood sample and we'll get the results in a few days. I'll put you back on medication – a mild sedative which you'll probably need for the rest of your life."

He explained to me that there were medications that alcoholics could safely take, but others such as valium, serapax and tryptanol were dangerous and would lead an alcoholic back to drink.

A week later, I returned for the test results. I was apprehensive, convinced that my liver would be shot to pieces and that I would not have long to live.

When I walked in, he looked at me without saying a word.

Taking this as an ominous sign, I asked, "How long have I got?"

He shook his head. "Geordie, your liver is in perfect condition. I can't believe it!"

Neither could I. I could not speak.

"I thought at first", he continued, "that the pathologist had made a mistake, so I queried his report, but he confirmed it. There is nothing wrong with your liver!" He smiled at me encouragingly. "You should go down in the Medical Journal as a miracle!"

While I was there, he gave me a thorough checkup. "You'll live a long time yet if you look after yourself. But it is up to you. I have watched many of your Skid Row friends die horrible deaths. I hope you don't end up the same – – you've been close to it many times before."

Now I was faced with the biggest problem of my life and it was not alcohol. It was me.

I was then in the forty-third year of my life. I had been drinking for twenty five of them, ten on Skid Row. I had endured an abnormal childhood and experienced a failed marriage. Extensive damage, mental and spiritual as well as physical, had been done. Had I not had the examples in A.A. of men and women miracles, who had been elevated from the same and worse personal hells as myself, I would not be sane enough to function now, let alone write this book. God, in His mercy, had provided living proof, by the examples of these people, that, ONE DAY AT A TIME I could also rise from the ashes.

Today, I can see the extent of the damage. I had been full of hate, trusting no-one, a danger to myself and those around me. But, I thank God for the members of A.A. in Sydney and especially Newcastle for their kindness, patience and tolerance. For the last four years of my drinking, these sober-alcoholics* had done everything to help me until, finally, most had, like the doctor, the hospital staffs, the police, ministers and a lot of others who had been in contact with me, despaired of me ever becoming sober and expected to read my obituary in the paper.

But now, these members of A.A. somehow knew that this was 'the time'. "He's got a chance. We think he'll make it!"

They rallied round, protecting me. I needed their help as

* There is no such person as an ex-alcoholic or a cured alcoholic. As alcoholism is an incurable disease, sobriety only arrests it.

I faced reality and tried to cope with my emotions. Could I live in a strange world without alcohol? I knew I could. The examples were always there. I thank God for these men and women who wanted nothing of me but to see me get well. The only repayment? "Pass it on to someone else whenever the opportunity arises."

I attended A.A. meetings every day and started looking around the churches. I was looking for something but did not know what it was. I got a small flat, found a job and slowly started to live what other people thought was a normal life, but inside there was a terrible turmoil and there were many times I wanted to drink, but I recalled where I had come from and I never wanted to go back there. Never!

The driving force that kept me sober for the first year was hate. I even hated the members of A.A. I hated society. I was determined that these bastards would never have the pleasure of seeing me drunk again! Determination and hate saved me whenever I despaired. Many times, on my own at night, I cried, praying to God – the God I did not understand – that he would give me the courage to hang on.

During the first months I would go back to my flat, sit on the bed and cry with loneliness and frustration. I did not want to mix with people or go anywhere. I could not watch television, go to dinner or a movie or any of the things normal people did. A.A. members gave me strength, explaining what was happening, that I was re-adjusting and beginning to come to terms with my new life. I went to church occasionally, but I had to go to A.A. for it was these people who were holding me together.

My reactions were sometimes frightening. On many occasions I screamed aloud and other times I cursed God. I wanted someone to share my life. I needed love. I had plenty to give but no-one to give it to. I still had the memory of Cathy with me. I felt she had rejected me and one night at an A.A. meeting which we were both attending, I threatened to take her life and she knew, as I did, that in my present state, I was capable of doing it.

Fearfully, I went to a member and told him about it. I told him I thought I would have to leave Newcastle. I also went to

Watt Street and spoke to one of the counsellors who had nursed me through my suffering.

I asked him if I would I be running away from my responsibilities if I left Newcastle knowing that I would continually run into Cathy at meetings.

I could not handle it and knew I could threaten her life again and I knew she was frightened.

The counsellor agreed that it would be a wise move to leave. "If anything gets in your way or upsets you, get away from it. Go to Sydney. Stay away until you are strong enough."

I remembered too, the advice of years earlier in Western Australia when A.A. members had told me to leave my family until I was strong enough to go back to see them.

So I went to Sydney. I had been in big cities before – Perth, Melbourne, Brisbane, Adelaide, Darwin – but I was always drunk and the size of the city and the loneliness did not bother me. I had always had my comforter, the bottle.

Sydney was big and lonely. I got a job, a flat and again, when I knocked off, I would sit down and cry in absolute loneliness. And I could not stay in a job. Being a brickie, a job was always easy to find. Looking in the paper, I would take note of three or four jobs in the same area. I could not trust myself to stay on a job. Often, I would start on a job at seven o'clock and be gone by eight. Having noted another job in the paper, I would start there. One day, I started on three different sites. I could not hold a job or mix with other people.

From what A.A. had taught me, I realized that I was trying to run things my way and that things did not work like that. I realized that in Sydney, a lot of people were self-taught bricklayers. Their poor workmanship irritated me and I had to run the job for them. I had to learn that this sort of reaction was wrong, but how was I to fix it? I would think, "Oh God! I'm never going to change," and I would cry with frustration. I was explosive, wound up like a spring. I couldn't even sit still. I was a walking time bomb, uneasy, impatient, intolerant and very dangerous. On building sites, I would throw things around. One day I threw a brick at a man from a high scaffold and just missed him. I knew I was capable of killing somebody. I prayed about it.

The damage had been done before I started drinking and I had used alcohol to bury it. The results were showing themselves and I was realizing that anger and hate were the biggest defects that I had been left with. I prayed to rid myself of them. One moment I would be as high as a kite and then for no apparent reason, in a deep depression. I called it the Agony and the Ecstasy of becoming sober. The members of A.A. had warned me of these things. They gave me glimpses of what would happen to me on the way. I believed them. On the way down, they had pointed out all the signposts and that if I continued to drink, I would pass them all. They had been right in every single instance, so I had to believe them on the difficult road to recovery. God would not give me more than I could bear for one day. I believed it and sometimes when I didn't think I could make it, I would hold on for just one more day. I would remind myself, too, of the days in the cells and empty houses, hopeless and sick.

"Just hang on Geordie. Just hang on a minute at a time. This won't last for ever. It will stop or you will die. Nothing lasts for ever."

Then came the happiest day of my life. I had been sober for twelve months. I had looked forward to this day every day in my attempt to stay sober. In A.A. it is called our First Birthday. Because I had tried to get sober in Newcastle and because the people there had helped me so much, I went back to celebrate my First Birthday as a token of my gratitude.

First, I went to see Dr Chandler. I walked into his surgery beaming and happy. I could not wait to tell him the good news.

"I've been sober for twelve months", I said, proudly.

He looked at me across his desk with a funny expression on his face and said, "I don't believe you."

I thought he was joking. "What do you mean, you don't believe me? Why should I lie to you?"

He said, "I don't believe you, Geordie, because you conned me for four years. I haven't seen you for about nine months, you walk in here and expect me to believe THAT!"

This flattened me. I had gone into that surgery in such a state of elation. I wanted to share my happiness with him, but he just sat there as though nothing had happened.

"When you've been sober for five years, I might believe it."

Although deeply hurt, I realized that I had made some progress, because I could handle it.

I said to myself, "It doesn't matter. You know and God knows. That is all that really matters."

The people of Newcastle were beautiful! I had gone up there to spend half a day with them and share with them my First Birthday in A.A. I stayed there four days. They would not let me get away. They invited me to their homes.

One man, with tears in his eyes, said, "Geordie, you're an absolute miracle."

Later, when I was strong enough, A.A. dropped a bomb on me. I was told that the average member takes three to five years to get well and stable, but for me, with my background, it would probably take five to seven years. I nearly fell through the floor! They were having a go at me. Why did I have to do the extra two years?

Today, I can see the wisdom of what they were saying. When I look back over my tumultuous life, I realize that God wasn't going to unscramble it in five minutes – that these things take time.

When I had been sober for sixteen months, I decided to go back to Western Australia to see my children. I had not seen them for eleven years. I worried about it and spoke to members of A.A. Was I ready for this? They assured me that I was, so, apprehensive, I boarded the plane.

My eldest son, Robbie, was at Perth Airport to meet me, having driven 254 miles from Albany. It was his twenty first birthday. The last time I had seen him, he had been ten years old. For eleven years, I had carried a picture in my mind of my children as I had last seen them. And here was Rob, a big, strong man, twice my size. The little boy was gone! He was a grown man!

He threw his arms around me and said, "Glad to see you."

During the drive back to Albany, I related a few of the incidents that had happened to me. He said, "Please don't tell me any more. It hurts too much."

In Albany, we went to my wife's house where four of my children were waiting for me. I was very frightened. Veronica, Belinda, Danny and Shaun were there. Christine, the eldest, was away with her husband. I stood in the kitchen of that house and looked at them and they looked at me. They were all adults, the image of them as little children smashed. It was a traumatic experience – we were all total strangers!

They said, "Good-day."

I replied, "Good-day."

That was all we could say and I wanted to run. I said to Rob, "I've got to go." I wanted to get out of there. I could not handle it.

Rob said to me, "Dad, give it time."

He had arranged for me to stay with my mother-in-law, just around the corner. I said to him, "Please take me around to your grandmother's place."

Rob was having his twenty first birthday party that night and had told his friends that his father was coming home. I knew this, but was frightened because I did not know how I would behave. I was still a bombshell. I was frightened that something might be said and that I would blow up and destroy the whole thing. In those days, when I was angry, I could become maniacal. I felt guilty too, because for eleven years, I had not supported them. How could I explain that to them?

I recalled too, that my mother-in-law had never liked me and had warned her daughter not to marry me. Yet, I was going to stay with her and my son had told me that she was happy to have me!

I thought, "Here's a set-up. She'll get me there and tear me to pieces."

She was eighty years old. She put her arms around me and crying, said, "It's good to see you. You can stay here. I'll be happy to have you." Then she added, "I feel sorry for you."

I said, "Don't feel sorry for me, Mum. Feel sorry for your daughter."

I dressed carefully for the party that night. I am immaculate when dressed. When I got there it was swinging and everybody was having a few beers. Rob made me feel welcome and introduced me to his friends. I felt relaxed with them, but with my other children it was difficult. I tried to make conversation with them. My youngest son, Danny, was only eighteen months old when I had last seen him and now he was thirteen.

Sitting in the kitchen, talking small talk to them was an uncomfortable experience. We were total strangers. And then, my youngest daughter, Belinda, came in and gave me an envelope.

She said, "Open this, Dad."

Inside was a 'welcome home' card and she had written on it, "We all love you, Dad. Welcome home!"

I cried, she cried, in fact we all cried a little bit. The card had broken the ice. I was able to relax and feel more comfortable.

I stayed in Albany for five weeks, but I was restless to get back to Sydney. I had left my A.A. friends behind and felt like a duck out of water. Albany was too small for me. I missed life in Sydney and I wanted to go back. Shaun and Rob decided to return with me.

In Sydney, we settled in the house and then the trouble started. The old 'me' came back. The old 'me' was ALWAYS there. I could not handle it. I knew the boys loved me but felt guilty and not deserving of their love and care.

Two or three months later, Veronica, my second daughter, joined us. I now had three of my children living with me.

Looking back today, I can see why I used to blow up and scream at them. It was not that I did not love them. It was not only the terrible feeling of guilt, but unknown to me, I was trying to push them away.

On one occasion, Veronica said to me, "Dad, I'll iron your shirt."

She really meant it. I saw the look in her eyes, but I said, "No, love. I'll iron it. Don't worry."

It was guilt that made me reject her. I did not deserve my girl ironing my shirt or washing my clothes. I had never done anything for her. I could not explain to her what alcohol had done; how it was responsible for breaking up our family; how it totally obsessed me.

I took them to a couple of A.A. meetings in the hope that they might understand, but they couldn't and I couldn't expect them to.

I fought with them. The boys would work on jobs with me and I would kick bricks and mortar boards off the scaffold, abuse the boss and shout at my two sons. Then, at home, I would think, "This is futile. I'm not getting anywhere. I'm not getting better."

I discussed it with members of A.A. They would encourage me and say, "You're doing the right thing, Geordie. You are not drinking! Don't have the first drink and you will get well."

I was two people. One was trying to be a decent person while the other kept trying to revert back. It was tormenting and frustrating. I needed a lot of faith. I had to believe what the members of A.A. had taught me. I also had to believe in God and that He was looking after me. These were the two things I had to believe in.

In one of these fits of torment, I went to see Steve, a man who I looked upon as my adviser and mentor.

He said, "Geordie, some are singed by alcohol, some suffer first degree burns, some second degree, and some third degree. You, Geordie, have suffered third degree burns and the healing process is going to take a long time. Slowly the wounds will heal, the tissues will mend, but the scars will be there for the rest of your life. You will learn to live with them but it is going to take time and you will suffer a lot of turmoil. You are going to be high and you are going to be low, but rely on God and A.A. Don't have one drink and you will get well.

That was the sort of encouragement I got – and still get.

I would ask Steve, "How long will this last?"

He would reply, "Hang on, Geordie and it will pass. If you take one drink, you may never find out."

My mind, I discovered, was like a computer. In a computer there are two digits, but one of mine was wrong. The wrong one was called 'alcohol' and my computer-brain had been trying to work with a wrong digit in it. This is impossible. It could not make correct computations. When I stopped drinking, the defective digit had been removed and slowly the members of A.A. replaced it with the right one. But the computer became confused trying to get used to the two right digits. My brain would go round and round. I would put questions in there and I could not get the answers. Now I understood why and slowly my brain was starting to work, but I had to keep feeding it with good information.

When I met Christine, I had been sober for eighteen months and she for about six months. With typical alcoholic determination and in spite of what we had been taught, we were going to make the relationship work. She was beautiful, petite and sixteen years my junior.

But it was not easy. It was natural that I should know more about alcoholism and life than she. I had been at both longer, but she could not accept this and tried to put me down. I attempted to explain that it was not a competition and I had to be careful what I said. This put pressure on the relationship. I suggested that we should keep it simple and just enjoy each other. I wanted to marry her.

When we met, we were both living in Sydney but she soon moved to Wagga. She had two children and was looking for a place in the country. It meant we would have to split up. From the beginning, we both knew that it was not going to work, even though we wanted it to. There was too much turmoil and we fought continuously.

When she went to Wagga, I remained in Sydney, both intending never to see each other again. We knew this to be vital for our own sobriety, but it was not long before we started to contact each other by phone and eventually I moved to Wagga.

I got a house, a job and got back with Christine. We both thought that this time it would be different. We would make it work, but it was not long before we were arguing again.

And then the unbelievable happened! We had talked about getting married and that somehow, someday we might be able to buy a small house. Of course, the idea of me ever getting a house was laughable. All I had was a concrete mixer, a wheelbarrow, a couple of shovels, an old ute, a few clothes and about $500 in the bank. Getting my own home was too ridiculous to think about.

But Christine would look through the local papers and point out properties to me – little houses ranging from $10,000 to $15,000. Even these were out of the question.

I would say, "Chris, we haven't even got the price of the front door knob, let alone the house." I would let it go at that.

But she was a goer, full of vitality and, unbeknown to me, was doing her own research.

I was working on a job one day when she arrived and said, "The bank is going to lend us $15,000."

I laughed. "You must be joking! Who's going to lend us $15,000?"

"Well, you come to the bank with me tomorrow and see the manager." She sounded smug.

Next day, very sceptical, I entered the manager's office with her. The Manager told us he would give us what he called an unsecured loan.

"You two deserve one. You have worked hard. I'll let you have the money. You go and buy yourselves a little place somewhere."

Christine soon found it in the small town of Illabo about thirty five miles away. It was in the middle of nowhere, a one horse town. There was a pub, a post office, a store and a population of about fifty. It was very isolated.

The cottage was built of weatherboard, lined inside with 6" pine boards. It sat on three acres of land. Being in the building trade, I looked at it and saw the potential, especially at $10,000. I knew that in Sydney, you could not get a garage built for $10,000. So we bought it.

The night we moved in, I walked around the back in the dark and fell to my knees. "God", I said, "I don't know why you've given me this house but it is a miracle! I've only been out of Skid Row for three years and here I am with a house!"

Not long after we moved in, I began to drink. It was a disaster. I had been sober for three years and I picked up a drink! It shattered me. The progression of the disease of alcoholism had got hold of me as I had been taught in A.A. Even if you stop drinking, the disease still progresses.

Once again, I proved what they had taught me, because I drank for five days, was in hospital for five days and during all those ten days, I was blacked out. I do not remember anything. All I remember is going to the hotel in Illabo and drinking that first beer. This is the progression of alcoholism and indicated to me how close I was to becoming a victim of Korsacoff's Syndrome, made manifest by my total loss of memory.

I did not give myself a chance of becoming sober again because I had seen too many people in A.A. who had stayed sober for a period, had had a drink and never gone back to A.A. and had died. This was the dilemma that faced me. Picking up that drink had taken me right back to square one.

But I remembered what the members of A.A. had taught me. "Geordie, you are a human being. You are not God. You make mistakes. You must pick yourself up and start again."

I prayed. I hung on and stayed sober for three months before I drank again. On this occasion I was in Sydney as Christine had moved back there. I had deserted my house in Illabo and followed her. I was to do this on many occasions – up to Sydney, back to Illabo. Either Christine would be coming to Illabo or I would be driving the 275 miles to Sydney. Picking up that drink in Illabo had brought back the insanity of alcoholism and I was driving all over the country, chasing her.

After that drink in Sydney, I drank for five days. Christine put me into Betric Hospital where I stayed for five days. Of those ten days I could not remember one! When I came out of the blackout, I was in Christine's car and she was driving me home.

I did not want to go back to the life I had lived. I still had Christine, as shaky as the relationship was. I still had A.A. and my God to hang on to. One day at a time I could get sober again, although, realistically, I gave myself little chance.

I went to see Steve. He was a lovely, kind man who had been sober for eighteen years. He had been through the mill and knew what I was up against.

He said to me in a gentle voice, "Geordie, you were sober for more than three years and you got well and strong. If you can get through this one, you will be ten times stronger and although it will be ten times harder you will be a ten times better person."

This gave me courage. I thought deeply, knowing where the trouble lay. It was my relationship with Christine. It was too powerful and neither of us could handle it. After the fights, I would always go back to the little place at Illabo. It was an isolated house and on the wall I had hung a picture of Jesus.

Every time I walked in the door, I would put my suitcase on the floor, look at the picture and say, "This is where You want me, isn't it? I know that Christine and I are not good for each other. Even though we've tried, we both know it is not going to work. You are trying to help us."

In my heart, I knew, and she knew that eventually we would

have to break the relationship, but neither of us had the courage. We could draw the best and the worst out of each other. In desperation, in this lonely place, I would get on my knees, look up at the picture and say, "Please give me the strength and the courage to stay here by myself. Perhaps, one day at a time, and with your help, I can do it."

But a couple of days later, Christine would ring from Sydney and, despite all my good intentions, my promises to God and to myself, I would not hesitate to pack my bag, throw it in the ute and drive straight down to Sydney. I would stay there for a week or two and after the usual tempest drive back to Illabo. This went on for two years. It was so futile and we both knew it, although strangely enough, I did not drink through all this turmoil.

On my knees at the shack, I would pray the same prayer: "Give me the courage to stay here."

But I could not bear to lose Christine. I loved her so much.

I can see now that it was my background that was slowly destroying her love for me. At times, I doubted that she loved me at all but I know she must have done, otherwise she could never have tolerated the crazy person that was me. I realize now how frustrated and helpless she must have felt at times. She was a lovely person.

Eventually, God gave us both the courage to make the break. That day I put my arms around her and holding her, said a prayer. "Please God, give us the courage to do what we have to do. I love Christine. Please take care of us both."

Christine looked at me and said, "Geordie, if you ever want me, look inside your heart and I'll always be there."

Once again, the person I loved was to be taken away from me and again, my world collapsed. It smashed me completely inside and I did not want to go on. For the first time in my sober life, I felt absolutely defeated.

I could not go back to Illabo in this terrible state. I knew it would be suicidal. I needed support, so I left Sydney and went to Newcastle where I knew I could get help. I stayed there six months.

I had been sober for nine months the second time round, but my mental condition was much worse than the first time.

I was not only trying to remain sober, I was also endeavouring to deal with my smashed emotions. Once again, I started to curse God. I became suicidal and even homicidal. The terrible hate that more than three years of sobriety had subdued had once again reared its head with added voracity. I knew I was going mad and so did my friends in A.A. On two occasions they got me to a doctor who prescribed sedatives. Work came to a halt and I did not give a damn for anything. I had lost Christine and had nothing to live for. Suicide seemed the only way out.

And then I was struck by a new experience. I found myself in a bad state of the DTs when I was cold sober! I was working eighteen miles from home when it happened. Driving home in that condition was difficult and dangerous and I prayed to God all the way.

I arrived shaking and crying. The thought of Christine was driving me mad. Choking with emotion, I stood in front of the picture of Jesus and screamed at it, "Please help me!"

On a small table nearby was a bible I had bought for 20 cents from a secondhand shop two weeks earlier. I opened it now for the first time, looking at the picture of Jesus as I did so. It fell open at the story of Job which I had never read before. It was the story of a rich man who had lost everything but because he did not lose his faith in God, all his possessions and more were returned to him.

Before I was halfway through that story, I was smiling. I said, "Thank you, God, for helping me. Perhaps this is what is happening to me."

I stayed in Newcastle for six months, going to A.A. meetings and visiting the sick alkies at Morriset Hospital, where I had been so many times as a patient. This was a great help in holding my mind together. I had to pray every day. I prayed, not to stay sober but to stay sane.

I knew the day was approaching fast when I would have to go back to the shack at Illabo and it was the last place I wanted to go to. There were too many memories of Christine there. To avoid going back, I tried on two occasions to sell it, but the prospective buyers could not raise the finance. Deep down, I knew that God had something to do with it. He was sending me back.

Again, I was on my own in the little house in the middle of nowhere and the pub only five hundred yards away! Even in the mental state I was in, I knew I had to make a decision. I could fill the house with booze, lock the windows and doors, tear the phone out of the wall and slowly drink myself to death, or I could turn that broken-down place into the dream house Christine and I had planned together.

I had no choice. I believed that there is a hell of some sort and that I would have to stand before God when I died. If there is no God or hell then I would lose nothing. If there is, I would have lost everything, forever, and if hell is just a tiny bit worse than what I was going through, I did not want to go there. It was safer for me to bear this, one day at a time, with the help of God and what I had been taught in A.A. With little will to go on, short of money, no job and with few prospects of getting one, I knew I could not give up.

Words of kindness offered to me by members of A.A. came back to me.

John R. had said, "God trusts you to carry this burden. He gives the heaviest cross to those He loves the most."

I thought, "He must certainly love me!"

"You are a good example to a lot of people", John had continued. "They know your pain and what you are going through. They have their eyes on you. If you go under with this load, some sick people will go too. Remember, Geordie, He won't give you any more than you can bear in one day."

Garry from Morriset had put his arm around my shoulder and said, "Whatever you do, don't for one minute, take your eyes off Him. If you do, you'll go under. He is the only one who can help you in this sort of pain. Stay very close to Him."

Lennie and Cherie had said, "We are all praying for you, Geordie. Trust God."

Blonde Carol, Marie, the patients at Morriset, Shearer Jack and Little Danny all said, "You have helped a lot of people. We will pray for you."

All these people were tough cases, hardened by life and booze. They had been through life's mill. They had been locked up, knifed, shot at, kicked and bashed and like me, had been driven to the point of despair. They knew it was God and no-one else who could carry us through these trials.

As difficult and as painful as it would be, I would stay and renovate the house. After many years in the building industry, I knew the physical task that faced me and how much it would be enlarged by my mental and spiritual condition, but my defiance and determination would prove to be strong assets.

I locked it in my mind, that no matter how long it took, no matter the pain, I would remain until the task was completed. I had known for a long time and had been taught by A.A. that in order to get well, I would need time on my own. This, then was the time. I wished it could have been under different circumstances.

For the first five months, I went to A.A. two or three times a week. Otherwise, I would have gone mad. Sleep was nearly impossible. I had sedatives, but was reluctant to take them. On many occasions, I worked right through the night, moving like a robot, praying, crying, trying to control my thoughts and telling myself to just keep going. Christine was always in my thoughts and I had to constantly remind myself that she was not going to come back.

"You won't get a letter or a phone call today", I kept telling myself. "There's nothing you can do about it except get on with your life." I had to repeat this over and over again and I was praying and cursing at the same time. It was cruel and I wanted out.

Every morning, I sat for half an hour to pray and meditate on the teachings of A.A. I forced myself to do this. I knew it was good discipline, hard self-discipline that I had never practised before.

Sometimes, I would get a small job outside, but the thought of mixing with other people terrified me. It was only the need for money for materials and the need to eat that forced me to do it. Although work at home and outside exhausted me physically and mentally, it kept me sane. Often I would go to pieces and breakdown and cry. On one of these occasions, I phoned Shearer Jack who lived on the Central Coast of N.S.W.

In a kind, gentle voice, he said, "Leave that shack, Geordie. Come back to us before you go insane. You can't survive there on your own. Can you drive, Geordie? If you can't, I'll come and get you."

Such was the love and concern of this man that he was prepared to drive the eight hundred mile round trip. I drove and when I arrived, Jack immediately took me to a doctor who wanted to hospitalize me in Sydney.

I refused the suggestion for two reasons. First, Christine was in Sydney and second, I knew that if I relied on God, He would protect me, even though I doubted this many times. I stayed with Jack for two weeks and got myself together before driving back to Illabo.

After several months, I decided that I must mix with other people and filter back into life. This was a disciplinary move. I did not want to make the effort. I wanted to hide myself away in this lonely house, away from everybody. People make you cry and I had cried enough already. But I had to make the attempt. So I joined the Wagga R.S.L. Club and travelled there every Saturday night.

The first nights were difficult. I would stay for an hour or so, then leave, driving the thirty five miles home in a deep depression. Back home, I would put on my working clothes and start work again. Sometimes, this would be eleven or twelve o'clock at night.

I continued to go to the R.S.L. and slowly, very slowly, I started to dance. I am a good dancer and consequently, I got to know some people, though always with my guard up. Women would compliment me on my dancing and this would raise my self-esteem.

I also started to attend a little church in Illabo. I went only to find out what God had to say. I would not talk to or mix with the people, though I became friends with the Minister and his wife. They were kind and friendly. We discussed the bible but they could not give me what I needed. I did not look at my bible often, but when I did it was to read Psalm 23. From this, I would get some measure of comfort but the only real reassurance I had was that God would take care of me.

Then I had the 'Experience'. I still do not understand it.

Always when I prayed to God, there would be a tiny, beautiful white light in my head, like a bright star and when it appeared, I knew I had contact. One night, as I lay in bed saying my prayers, this small white light appeared. It got bigger and bigger until it engulfed me with its brilliance, a white I had never seen before or since. It resembled the sun shining on rain falling gently through the clouds. I knew it was the power of God. To this day, I do not understand it and only occasionally do I get glimpses of it.

A lady, Val, an alkie I had met at A.A. meetings during my days in Newcastle, came to stay with me for a few days. I was glad to have her companionship. One night, we went to Wagga, and feeling depressed, I bought a heap of booze – enough to kill me, whisky, wine, beer – and put it in the car.

I wanted to drink it immediately, but knew that if I took one drink I would not be able to drive the thirty five miles home. I had Val with me too, and had no right to put her in danger.

On the way home, I knew that as soon as I arrived, I would get the top off the whisky bottle and end it all. I believe that every alkie of my calibre knows when they have had their last chance. I had had mine and I knew that to take one drink would be fatal. I would lose either my life or my sanity, but I did not care. I had lost Christine and there was nothing to live for. God had locked me in this little house miles from anywhere. What would He do to me next? I was not going to hang around to find out. Eighteen months sober and this, my second time round, did not count for anything.

As soon as I got home, I filled a large glass with whisky, sat down and took a mouthful. I can recall the look of terror on Val's face. In desperation and with tears in her eyes, she rang one of my friends in A.A.

I heard her say, "Please come straight away. Geordie is going to die!" She put the phone down and turning to me, said, "Wagga Mike will be here in forty five minutes."

I knew him well. He was a dear friend.

I continued to hold the whisky in my mouth. All I had to do was swallow it. I knew that if I did, it would be the end. In my semi-demented mind, I said, "Please God, help me."

In an instant, Skid Row was put before me and I clearly heard, "I got you sober and gave you a second chance. I've looked after you until now. You swallow that and you will be damned for ever!"

I spat out the whisky and asked Val to get me three sedative pills, knowing they would knock me out in a few minutes.

I know, had I not called God at that moment, I would be dead today. He was protecting me from myself and understood my helplessness.

How long I slept, I do not know, but it was Mike who woke me. The three of us sat in the kitchen with the cargo of booze on the table. Mike spoke words of encouragement and looking at the booze, said, "Geordie, you don't need this, do you?"

"No, Michael", I said. "Take it with you."

Val left Illabo the next day.

Slowly, I found a little strength and at times, a little peace. Gradually, I was learning my emotional limitations. I was beginning to understand the damage my past life had caused – the life before I had ever picked up a drink. The initial damage had not been done by alcohol but it had intensified the worst defects of my character – hate, anger, mistrust. Those Nuns, Priests and Brothers had done a brilliant job of twisting my mind. They were experts at that.

Slowly and painfully I learned. I read books when my mind was stable enough, which was not very often. One book I read, "Walking With Loneliness", helped me. Loneliness, I learned is as much a part of life as happiness, sorrow or any other emotion and that much is to be learned from it. One could make it a time of dread or use it to one's advantage. Loneliness brought me close to God and nature and made me more aware of myself and my friends. Loneliness is not something to be frightened of as though it is a sickness. It was described as entering into a dark, spiritual cave and if one had the courage to walk through the opening, one would get self-knowledge and spiritual knowledge and the further one went into the cave, the darker and more frightening it would become, but the knowledge gained would be worth the experience. This made a lot of sense to me. It brought me to an awareness of myself. I utilised it then and still do today. Without loneliness, I would never have grown.

I was becoming aware of the benefits of self-discipline. It was making me a stronger person. By this time I had been at the house about sixteen months. It was nearly finished but I did not care. I still wanted Christine back. But I had made up my mind to finish the place. I would not be beaten. Nobody or anything else would ever beat me. I had made that vow the night I ran away from Bindoon.

But today, I realize that there are three things that can defeat me – God, myself and alcohol.

I was still going to the R.S.L Club every Saturday night and having one-night stands with women. I was getting to know a lot of them, but I did not want to settle with anyone. I would be driving the thirty five miles home from the Club in the middle of winter, sometimes at four or five o'clock in the morning and thinking what a waste of time it all was for a few hours dancing and a few hours in bed with a woman. It was crazy. For a few hours of what passed for happiness, I was doing a seventy mile trip in the freezing cold, spending money I could not afford and missing my Church service on Sunday. I could be spending my Saturday nights at home by the fire, reading and improving my mind. I knew it would be hard to stop as it had become a way of life, but it was not making me happy and was of no benefit.

Not long after this, I watched a documentary on television and learned that Kepler had discovered that the universe is run by precise laws which are fixed and permanent and should any of them be interfered with, then the universe will be out of line. I thought about this deeply. If something as vast as the universe is governed by precise laws, then everything else connected with it must be too. I brought this down from the universe to this small planet and related these laws to the animals and plants. All had laws which, if broken, would mean that they would not survive. I was living on my own with nature and observed what went on around me. The birds and animals and plants were provided for; the sun came up every day; the rain fell when it was needed. I could see the peace and harmony of it. I was part of the universe and therefore, must be ruled by the same laws.

But where could these laws be found? The only place would be the Scriptures. I searched the bible and found, in Exodus, that God had laid down the laws for man to live in harmony with everything on the planet. He had told man, "If you do this, I will take care of you. If you do that, you must take the consequences."

It was clear. There it was, the moral code – what I could eat, what I could drink, how to live in harmony with the animals and the whole of nature. My life had obviously got into such a mess because I had thrown away the rule book. Here was another piece of the jigsaw. If I stopped fighting God, other people and myself, life would be much easier and like a leaf in the stream, I would just flow with the current. As a result, I became a lot calmer.

By now, I had finished renovating the house. It was beautiful. I was proud of it. I had also dug up the yard, planted lawns, rose bushes and trees. Then I became frightened. The work was running out. What could I do next to maintain my sanity?

I had always wanted to learn music and decided I would teach myself to play the piano, although I could not read a note of music and I did not have an instrument. But then I had a stroke of luck. One of the ladies at the Church sold me a beautiful German piano for $125. I had just enough to pay for it. To add to my delight, the lady was a music teacher and she gave me three lesson books and taught me how to use them. So for an hour every morning and evening, I would sit and struggle with the piano and the music books. My self-discipline was paying off.

I would put a clock on top of the piano and say to myself, "Welshie, you sit here for one hour and no smoking while practising."

It was not too difficult, because now my mind was coming together. I was able to cope with the loss of Christine and, in fact, this was simple compared to what I had already been through.

Then I remembered the words of many friends over the years. "Geordie, write your life story. You owe it to posterity, to yourself and to other people. It could help a lot of people." So I started to write this book. That was in 1983.

I knew what I had been through had been necessary; that without it I would never have become strong emotionally or spiritually and as a consequence, I was grateful for the pain. I was becoming a different person and I knew it.

I was working more now and saving some money. With much hard work and discipline, I had completed the manuscript in its rough form, had learned a few notes of music and decided it was time to leave.

Where would I go? I dare not go back to Sydney, because Christine was still there. Newcastle was too close to Sydney. I had my sister Maureen in Adelaide. I would go there. I packed the manuscript in my trunk.

I rented my house and left for Adelaide to begin a new life.

CHAPTER

7

Though the mills of God grind slowly,
Yet they grind exceeding small;
Though with patience He stands waiting,
With exactness grinds He all.
Friedrich von Logau, 1605-1655

I first wrote this book not long after I had stopped drinking. It was then a 400 page draft, which I considered a work of genius.

Friends and others who read it, kindly and diplomatically suggested it was raw, repetitive and required substantial editing, but I was adamant that I would not change a word! I was determined it would be published the way it was written or not at all. So I threw it into a trunk where it remained for two years.

On reading it again, it became obvious to me why I could not find a publisher. It was full of repetitive hate, anger and resentment towards Catholicism and I was disgusted with myself for having written it in such a bitter vein. So, moderating my dogmatic attitude, I sought professional advice and settled down to edit and rewrite the original manuscript. It was an onerous task, but I was finally rewarded when it was accepted for publication.

But what a revelation to the progress I had made on my painful journey of recovery. I was mellowing. Over four years, my thinking had changed dramatically and I had developed more tolerance, patience and understanding towards my fellow man. Anger and hate were slowly dissipating. I had to be on the right road.

Many times I recall the words A.A. members have told me over the years. "THIS WILL BE THE HARDEST THING YOU WILL EVER DO IN YOUR LIFE, BUT THE REWARDS WILL BE GREAT. THINGS WILL HAPPEN TO YOU BEYOND YOUR WILDEST DREAMS."

In this long, hard journey, I have shed many tears trying to readjust and face the realities of life. I have constantly struggled with my emotions, particularly aggression and my erratic moods.

Over these years, I have observed many people in A.A. who have been sober for two or three years and who appear to be leading normal lives, able to cope with their problems and emotions. Why couldn't I do the same? Regardless of my past life, I knew I should be far more emotionally stable. What was wrong? I prayed every day and asked for God's guidance, went to meetings of A.A. and tried to lead the A.A. way of life which simply means leading a decent life. I knew that what I was doing was honest and I was doing the best I could, but why wasn't I getting well? I know that over seven years, I have improved a thousand fold and my aggression is not one quarter as bad as in the past and my anxiety level is lower. I am grateful for this.

I had been told by the wise old members of A.A. that, although it takes three to five years for the average alcoholic to get well, for me it could be five to seven years. But I thought, that because of my childhood and past life, it could take me ten to fifteen years. Why hadn't I achieved a greater degree of mental stability? I must be doing something wrong, but what? The answer would come to me if I waited.

I was learning more about my cruel disease. I learnt that the disease of alcoholism is not in the bottle. If that was the case, everybody who drinks alcohol would become an alcoholic, but that is not so.

For many years, the medical profession has suspected a chemical imbalance in the make-up of the alcoholic and this has recently been proved. There is an imbalance in my chemical physiology and once having taken a drink, I am condemned to drink against my will.

Early in my alcoholism, I used to bury the fears and trauma of my childhood. I became aware of how my past had twisted all my concepts of spirituality, sex, morality, love and authority. A.A. taught me that, in order to recover, I had to undo everything I had learned and start all over again. What a task to undo nearly forty three years of learning!

I related alcoholism to the force of Evil whose sole purpose is to have people suffer and I have to be constantly on my guard, because the disease I am suffering from is cunning, baffling and patient. I must keep reminding myself of who I am and where I came from and who got me out of there, otherwise I would soon slip back.

The remedy is attending regular meetings of A.A. and developing an awareness of spiritual things. I had to learn to live a new life and at first, I did not know how. I found it difficult to speak and even understand the language used by A.A. members. They used strange words like 'please', 'thank you', 'do you mind' and 'we suggest'. These were alien words in my vocabulary, which consisted of profanities and Skid Row jargon.

They also spoke of God and that frightened me. Another bunch of religious cranks, I thought. And then they pointed out to me – GOD AS YOU UNDERSTAND HIM. This allowed me to make a God of my own choosing and gave me some sense of freedom in that area.

Looking back to those early days, I was insane and there was a lot of damage done. I was often frightened and felt like a little boy locked in a dark room who could not find the light switch or the door. The members of A.A. would turn the light on and lead me by the hand, as though I were a small child, saying, "This way, Geordie." They are still doing it and I will always need their guidance. I have to go to them constantly to find the answers – the answers I need to walk this strange road of sobriety. I need to be reassured that I am on the right track as the thought of going back to Skid Row horrifies me.

But a greater horror than that is the knowledge that, if I pick up another drink, I will have to stand before God and answer to Him. I know it would be the ultimate price – a price I am not prepared to pay.

In the early days, I hated the members of A.A. and was very defiant, but they and they alone, had the answers. Slowly over the years, I have had to temper my defiance and listen to people, not only in A.A., but in all walks of life. I had to humble myself and realize that other people were intelligent too and that, if I exposed myself to them and kept an open mind, I could learn from them and make this painful walk easier.

Living in Adelaide, I had a lot of contact with my sister, Maureen, whose childhood was similar to mine and I was able to see in her the damage that had been done to me.

Like me, Maureen had an escape route. She did not use alcohol; she used pills. For a long time, she spoke only of her childhood, and then with hate and aggression. Observing this was helpful, because it indicated to me that I had come a long way and that carrying a chip on the shoulder was futile. It had been destroying my life for years and I could now see that it was doing the same for Maureen. I spent many hours talking to her about the uselessness of such thinking. I pointed out that the people responsible were probably dead and that they had had to account to God for the damage they had done, and that it was unfair that the people we associate with today, should have to bear the brunt of our past. They were innocent. The past should not be allowed to control her life. She was always going to doctors to get different pills which only screwed her up more than ever.

My observations of Maureen indicated to me that I was on the road to recovery. Listening to her talk and watching her behaviour was like a mirror of my own past. Her reiteration of her life in the orphanage would upset me, as it revived memories long since buried. I explained to her many of the things I had been taught at A.A. I suggested that she must reconcile herself with the past and face reality without the use of chemical substances and until she did this, she would have no hope of getting well. My words, thank God, did not go unheeded. Now, three years later, she no longer takes drugs and leads a happy life.

Today, I am able to see the damage religion has done to me, my sister and countless thousands of people like us. Is it a coincidence that I can safely state that seventy five to eighty per cent of A.A, members are Catholic? My alcoholism is a fear-based disease and the basis of Catholicism is steeped in fear.

In this period of seven years, I have met my children on many occasions, though the relationship has been strained. I have tried to explain to them, without excuses, the nature of my disease and that it was responsible for the break-up of our family. But the damage has been done.

If I allowed it, this type of relationship with my children could get me down, but through examples in A.A., I realize there is nothing I can do about it. I live in the hope that what happened to a lot of my friends in A.A. who were in the same predicament, may happen to me. One day my children may come back. I still live in hope of this, although I have no expectations. Like many other things, this is in the hands of God.

Whilst living in Adelaide, my daughter Veronica came over to live with her boy-friend. She made contact with me and, of course, I was delighted. I trod carefully. Perhaps I could show this girl that I was a decent person; that I was not what ignorant people had told her. But I had to prove it.

She came to my flat once a week to clean it for me. It did not need cleaning. I was quite capable of doing it myself. But because I knew she was short of money, I paid her for doing it. The relationship between us was an easy one. She was a happy-go-lucky girl and seemed to hold no grudge.

Unfortunately for me, she stayed in South Australia for only three months before returning to the West. She had been away about twelve months when my eldest son, who was in New South Wales, rang me at six o'clock one Sunday morning to tell me that Veronica had taken her own life. I was stunned! I could not believe it! But I knew at that moment that I had to hold myself together.

"Veronica is dead", I told myself, "and there is nothing you can do about it. All your crying, praying, pleading will not bring her back."

I reminded myself of lines from Khali Gibran: "Your children are not your children ... they come through you, but not from you."

Putting the phone down, I immediately rang a member of A.A. I knew this action was imperative. This was a new factor and I did not know how I would react. My friend asked me to come straight over to his place. He spent several hours with me, encouraging me and telling me the reactions I would experience and how to cope with them. This was a traumatic time, but strangely, I had no desire to drink.

This was reality. This was life. People are born and people die. It was a law of the universe and because I was part of it, I came under these laws. I could be no exception. I put the tragedy to the back of my mind and got on with my life. I did not go back to Western Australia for the funeral as my friend in A.A. strongly advised me against it.

I decided that one day I would go back to the West, stand by my daughter's grave and say "Goodbye" in my own way.

Today, I have learned to live one day at a time; to cope with adversity and reality, as painful or as happy as they may be. In my journey, I have read many books and talked with many people. I have discovered that nobody can give me the answers to my spiritual questions. I have to search for and find them myself.

The Master said, "Believe no man. Do not even believe in Princes. Search the Scriptures for yourself and find your own truths."

I have found many of the pieces of the jigsaw; have realized that there are many mysteries that cannot be solved on this earth and which belong only to the realm of the Spirit and that my life is a constant search for Truth.

Weigh it up for yourself. If there is no God, if there is no power greater than you or I, how is it that today I can write this book, read philosophy, study art and music, cut marble and overcome seemingly hopeless situations. I am a respected member of society. I can function efficiently. In spite of the theories of doctors and psychiatrists, I have all my faculties. These well-meaning people in the medical profession had stated, categorically, "Geordie, should you ever stop drinking permanently, the damage you have done to your body is so extensive that you will never be able to perform normally again." In my fortieth year, they had even tried to pension me off!

Thank you, Lord, that I can smile. Please never let me forget why I cried.